CONFESSIONS OF A SEX DOCTOR

Books by Robert Chartham

SEX MANNERS FOR MEN (New English Library)
MAINLY FOR WOMEN
SEX MANNERS FOR ADVANCED LOVERS
SEX AND THE OVER-FORTIES
ADVICE TO MEN
ADVICE TO WOMEN
THE CHARTHAM LETTERS
THE *FORUM* GUIDE TO SEXUAL PROBLEMS
THE SENSUOUS COUPLE
etc, etc.

CONFESSIONS OF A SEX DOCTOR

Robert Chartham, PhD

NEW ENGLISH LIBRARY

A New English Library Original Publication, 1983

First NEL Paperback Edition October 1983

NEL Books are published by
New English Library,
Mill Road, Dunton Green,
Sevenoaks, Kent.
Editorial office: 47 Bedford Square, London WC1B 3DP

Photoset by Rowland Phototypesetting Ltd,
Bury St Edmunds, Suffolk

Printed in Great Britain by
Cox & Wyman, Reading

British Library C.I.P.

Chartham, Robert
Confessions of a sex doctor.
1. Sexual disorders—Case studies
I. Title
616.6′9 RC556

ISBN 0-450-05628-7

Contents

Introduction

THEORETICALLY, AND from an anatomical point of view, the functioning of our sexual apparatus should be no more complicated than any of our other natural functions – for example, the deflation and reflation of our lungs, the pumping of the blood through our bodies by the heart, the digestive processes of food by the stomach and its associated organs, the unconscious peristalsis of the colon which pushes the waste material from the food down towards the outside world via the anus, or the secretion of urine by the kidneys, the passage of the urine to the bladder and the emptying of the bladder during urination.

Leaving aside the procreative potential of the sexual conjunction of male and female, the physically pleasurable release of sexual tension, built up either through the action of hormones or by deliberate stimulation of external and internal sexually sensitive and responsive zones, is so attractive an experience that few who have discovered it once do not want to do so again. However, whether for procreative or purely sensational ends, certain physical conditions are needed for the body to express its sexual attributes at all. The male penis must be transformed from its unaroused flaccid state, into a stiff erection, and to do this it must be stimulated by rubbing against the interior of the vagina or the mouth, or by the hand or other means, such as a vibrator, to produce ejaculation of semen accompanied by orgasm. Similarly, stimulation of the clitoris is needed before erection and orgasm can be achieved by the woman.

One of the great differences between, say, urinating and defecating (which are both also accompanied by physically pleasurable sensations, though none of the quality of the sexual orgasm) and sexual response is that defecating and urinating sensations cannot be shared with another person, while the sexual function was primarily (procreatively)

designed to be an unavoidably shared experience. Even non-procreative sex, which does *not* involve penis–vagina contact, can be a shared experience by the mutual use of hands and mouths.

The sexually shared experience is greatly enhanced by the involvement of the other partner. Nevertheless, when both partners are motivated into sexual activity only by the sexual chemistry of the body building up a sexual tension requiring release, they indulge in an act of sheer lust, whatever it entails. But if an all-pervasive emotional interaction between the partners accompanies the sexual sharing – or is the motivator of it – then the act is one of love. Put very simply, it is this emotional intervention which creates the difference between lust and love.

Because the actual physiological requirements for the male to perform the sex act are so simple, and are even more simple in the case of the female (whose vagina can be entered, whether she is sexually roused or not, provided the penis is well lubricated), one would imagine that the shared sex act cannot fail to be successful. But the very same emotional responses which improve the quality of shared sex can also, contrariwise, prevent the essential, very simple transformations from taking place, thus making it impossible for a couple to share a satisfactory and satisfying sexual experience.

This involvement of the emotions in physical sexual experience has its source in the brain, and it is in the sexual function that the brain is seen to have a more direct influence than in any other bodily function. Admittedly, it is the brain that directs us to urinate when the sensations of a full bladder are communicated to it, for example, but it cannot – except in very very rare complicated cases – prevent us from urinating when the bladder will hold no more.

The brain, on the other hand, can have a complete control over our physical sexual functioning, for example, in the achievement of erection of the penis and the amount of stimulation required – either a little or a lot – to make it fully stiff, and therefore achieve ejaculation and orgasm;

and similarly the amount of stimulation of the clitoris – again, either a little or a great deal – required to bring the woman to climax.

No one who has not had the experience of dealing with the sexual difficulties experienced by men and women can, I believe, ever fully understand the power of control that the brain has over physical sexual function, not only in the individual generally, but also in the individual from one experience to the next.

Most men can achieve orgasm and ejaculation after an average of three to four minutes of direct stimulation after the penis has reached full erection. His partner, on the other hand, usually requires eight to ten minutes of direct stimulation of the clitoris to reach orgasm. From this it becomes apparent that if the brain, under pressure from one source of influence or another, prevents the man from controlling his 'speed to orgasm', his partner will never have any hope of reaching her orgasm during penis–vagina contact.

Fear of one kind or another, guilty feelings about sexual activity induced by religious precepts or by parents or others, nervousness and possibly previous experiences embedded in the subconscious but perpetually operating when the man or woman finds himself/herself in the ultimate sexual situation – all are the main causes of widespread sexual unhappiness.

Such inhibitions, as we call them, can be treated and removed, but only by people like myself – psychosexual therapists, who have studied psychology in general and specialised in the psychology of sexual dysfunction or malfunction. Many men and women do not realise that such 'sex doctors' exist, nor how they can be helped by them. Quite unnecessarily, they commit themselves, instead, to lives of sexual and emotional unhappiness.

It is in an attempt to draw attention to the help that is available that I have decided to recount some of my more unusual case histories, and how I was able to apply successful treatment.

The cases I have described here are nearly all unique, but

they do emphasise the power that the mind has over sexual functioning. By contrast, the great majority of cases have more simple origins and can be more easily treated, though they cause no less personal unhappiness. I urge any reader with a sexual problem to seek help because it is foolish to undertake a burden of unnecessary unhappiness and suffering.

If any reader with a problem would like to write to me, care of the publisher of this book, I will do all I can to advise him/her.

Finally, with the view of guarding completely the confidentiality between patient and doctor, all those figuring in these case histories have been so utterly disguised that they will only be able to recognise themselves through the description of the actual special problem described.

Robert Chartham

1 An Unusual Rape

FROM THE beginning I have made it a rule not to become sexually involved with my patients, and throughout 40 years of therapy I have broken this rule only about three times, and each time for a special reason, mainly because the case was unique or very rare and aroused my deep scientific interest. On the other hand, I have never had second thoughts about using surrogates – male and female – if I thought a solution to a problem would be found by this means.

I used to have quite a sophisticated clinic in London, which I later gave up when we went to live in Malta. It consisted of a reception-area-cum-waiting-room; a consulting-room, which contained an examination couch, two easy chairs, a low table and a desk; and a bathroom, leading off the consulting-room, in which there was a two-way mirror which gave full vision of the bedroom next door, especially the bed, where much of the action in some of my therapy took place. There was also a communicating door between the consulting-room and the bedroom, which was concealed by curtains on both sides, and which I only used in circumstances which required my personal intervention in the bedroom.

I had two female surrogates, both of whom were as skilled in the techniques of lovemaking as any women you could find. One, Sylvia, who also acted as my receptionist, I chose initially for her small breasts, while Margaret I chose for those men who are turned on by large breasts. But in terms of skill there was nothing to choose between them.

The same could be said of my male surrogates, whom I selected for build. George, who was 25, had a figure like Michelangelo's *David*, though his penis was quite a bit larger. He had a great sense of humour, too. He made his

living as a male prostitute, having a regular clientele of young, rich, sexually dissatisfied women and, as he was one of the most balanced bisexuals I have encountered, an equal number of male customers 30 years old and upwards.

George was very popular because he had a magnificent pubic bush and very thick axillary hair, but not much hair on his chest, which appeals to large numbers of women. He was popular with me because he was nearly always available on instant demand – and he would pass up one of his own clients if I asked for his help – and he also understood a good deal about male and female sexual psychology and dysfunction. When I discussed a case with him, I only had to give him a brief outline of the treatment I thought would help and he understood at once, and quite often he would come to me with suggestions.

For women who are turned on by very hirsute men, I could call on Martin, who had an almost ape-like pelt, front and back. He was a civil servant in the Department of the Environment, and could always take an hour away from the office at short notice. He was not quite so skilled as George, nor so sexually imaginative, but he was very intelligent and quickly assimilated any 'suggestions' I made to him. He was 30 and divorced, but he had rather an extravagant mistress so that he found the fees I paid him from time to time very useful.

Richard was a medium-height, thick-set man just nearing the end of his 40s. By profession he was an art dealer, but he had a very expensive taste in vintage motor cars and was always claiming to be on the verge of bankruptcy for that reason. He was popular with younger and older women, and did not mind which, so long as he got his fee – 'and, of course, a little bit of fun'. He could have made a number of worthwhile marriages if he hadn't loved his wife quite so much.

James was a well-preserved 65, very distinguished-looking when dressed, and perhaps even more distinguished-looking undressed. He was a widower who, after 30 or more years of a very happy marriage, didn't think he could find a replacement for his late wife, but 'wanted to

make women happy'. I used him with young women looking for a father-figure.

By the same token, I kept Eileen in reserve for young men who wanted a mother-figure or, as they would say, 'a mature woman who will understand my problem and take me seriously'. She was just coming up to the 'change', but had preserved her figure marvellously, especially her breasts at which she had suckled four children. Her husband was very proud of the fact she 'worked' for me. 'He always told me I had talent,' she said, with a twinkle in her eye, 'and now you've proved him right.' Eileen was also happy to help elderly men with what she called 'their lost vigour', by which she meant had difficulty in getting a firm erection.

For cases requiring specialist treatment, generally a particular size or shape of penis, I could call on George's 'escort agency', which had on its rolls a number of sexually well-equipped, handsome young West Indians, who especially appealed to some women who were attracted by dark skin, honey-like voices and sizeable 'fillings', and to others, among them 'women's libbers', who could only be turned on by domination fantasies incorporating black slaves. The beauty about George's retinue, black and caucasian, was that they were all highly professional. They were completely uninhibited and highly sexually imaginative. You could ask them to do whatever you thought would help, and they never hesitated, and they were all articulate so they, like George and the others, could write up case notes which were comprehensible.

But, in my opinion, George was the doyen of all my surrogates. He had the ability – which, in respect of time, I believe exceeded Maupassant's – of being able to achieve a full erection in ten seconds by psychological stimulation only, whenever required to do so.

He was very proud of this. 'Like to see my party piece?' he asked, grinning, at our first interview.

'If you'd like to show me,' I told him, wondering what on earth he intended to do.

So he stood up, dropped his trousers and his underpants

to reveal a completely flaccid penis. Then he began to count and I watched his penis swell and stiffen and stand up until it was tapping against his belly by the time he had reached ten.

'How do you do it?' I asked, fascinated.

'I don't know, really,' he said. 'I just say to it – without speaking, of course – stand up, you little fucker, and it stands up.'

Well, those were my assistants, some of whom you will be meeting in these case histories. However, before I begin to relate the first, I ought to tell you that when I was in consultation I wore only white (or green) trousers, held up by an elastic waist-band, a white (or green) tunic which zipped from the bottom to just above my navel, and white (or green) moccasins. The loose tunic and trousers provided me with a feeling of freedom which ordinary clothes do not, while white and green are 'professional' colours.

Right then! A short time ago, a certain sexologist wrote an article in which he suggested that some women experience difficulty in obtaining orgasm because they have a 'hooded clitoris'.

The clitoris, as you know, is analogous with the penis, except that, besides having no opening in the tip, it is very very small even when compared with the smallest penis, and its shaft lies permanently buried under the skin. Like the penis when the man is sexually aroused, the clitoris becomes erect when the woman is aroused, and in this condition its head emerges from a hood of skin which resembles the foreskin of the uncircumcised penis. The clitoris is a compact mass of nerves, most of which (as in the penis) are concentrated in the head. These nerves are an important part of the woman's sexual nervous system, to the extent that it is by stimulating the clitoris that the woman is brought to orgasm.

During foreplay, the woman is aroused by her partner using his penis or his tongue to stroke and caress the clitoris. When she enters her final phase of excitement and urges the man to penetrate her, the movements of his penis within her vagina, acting via the labia (the 'sex-lips'), draws the hood of the clitoris downwards over the clitoral head as

he thrusts inside her, and releases it as he pulls back. This backwards and forwards movement of the hood over the clitoral head stimulates the orgasm-sensation nerves to produce an orgasm.

It used to be thought by some sexologists that it was the stimulation of the clitoris by the shaft of the penis rubbing against it as the man thrust and withdrew that achieved the woman's orgasm, but there are very few couples so physically 'engineered' that the penis comes into contact with the clitoris after penetration has taken place. It was Masters and Johnson who observed the movement of the clitoral hood and thereby discovered how the clitoris is stimulated during coupling.

I think it must be common knowledge, but I must mention it nevertheless, that if the man's foreskin is not pulled back over the penis-head during childhood – but not until the child is at least three years old – and adolescence, he will not be able to pull it back when he has reached maturity. There are adhesions under the foreskin which can attach it firmly to the penis-head while, in addition, the opening in the foreskin cannot be stretched sufficiently to allow the penis-head to emerge.

Any man with an unretractable foreskin – or any woman whose partner has an unretractable foreskin – must *never* attempt to pull it back themselves. If they do succeed in getting it back – after much suffering on the part of the man – they may not be able to get it forward again, and this will lead to strangulation of the penis, a very, very serious condition in which the circulation of the blood is stopped, and immediate medical and surgical attention must be sought to save the penis from amputation.

Now, whereas the man with the unretractable foreskin can have an erection and be stimulated to orgasm and ejaculate in the ordinary way, if the woman's clitoral hood does not retract, she cannot be stimulated to orgasm during penetration by the hood sliding backwards and forwards over the clitoral head caused by the man's thrusting.

It would, therefore, seem very important to the woman's achievement of orgasm, if not outright indispensable, that

her clitoral hood should have absolutely free movement over the head.

This was what struck the sexologist whom I have mentioned, and as a result of his article and the taking up of this theory by others, for a time there was a kind of 'fashion' in England – and especially in London – for anorgasmic women to wonder whether they might not be the victims of 'The Hooded Clitoris'.

I had a number of requests for appointments from such women who, on examination, proved to be quite normal, except for the fact their clitorises were either abnormally small, and showed only the very tip even when fully erect, or else had clitorises of normal size but were so situated at the apex of very heavy sex-lips that they could not be easily seen by the woman inspecting herself with a mirror.

(By the way, the genuine hooded clitoris is extremely rare. During the last 15 years of professional practice, I have encountered only three, and the experience of colleagues supports mine. The hood that does adhere over the clitoris is easily released by a quick and very simple surgical operation – a series of small snips.)

Almost all the women who sought my advice presented me with no trouble at all. That is to say, when I asked them to remove their panties and lie on the examination couch, they complied without any hesitation or objection. The examination is brief, since it only entails the doctor parting the sex-lips with one hand, while he locates the clitoris with the fingers of the other, and gently draws back the hood to expose the head.

As I have just said, none of the women who asked me to examine them for a hooded clitoris gave any trouble at all until one afternoon Sylvia showed a Mrs X into my consulting-room.

Mrs X was a striking woman, with very black hair beautifully coiffeured, large brown eyes, a perfectly proportioned nose and thick, though not Negroid, lips. Her breasts were too large to be a personal turn-on for me, but I am sure they would inspire most readers of any 'girlie' magazine. Her hips were wide, the perfect hips for child-

bearing. Below her skirt appeared shapely calves which tapered down to neatly turned ankles.

She was 32, she told me when seated in the armchair opposite my desk. She had been married twice, and had been divorced for the second time only a few weeks previously.

'Both my husbands left me for other women,' she said, 'after complaining that beautiful though I might be, I was hopeless to make love to because they couldn't bring me off. They'd known that I was difficult to bring to climax, because I hadn't cheated on them before marriage, and each said he had been certain he could perform the miracle where others had failed, which was why he had married me.'

So far, so good! There are men like this who have such a good self-assessment of their sexual abilities – without having any psycho-sexual know-how – that they are confident that their techniques *must* succeed.

'Oh!' I said. 'You do know what an orgasm is?'

She laughed. 'Of course! I can give myself an orgasm and so can my partner if he follows my instructions.'

'And what are your instructions?'

'He must bring me off by stimulating my clitoris with his fingers. When he has done that, and if he enters me immediately, I get a great deal of satisfaction.'

'Did you not tell your husbands this?' I asked.

'I tried,' she sighed.

'And . . .?'

'They both said, "Leave it to me," which is what many of my lovers say.'

'Has any succeeded?' I asked.

'Of course! But I still haven't had an orgasm when my partner's penis has been in my vagina . . . and that is what I want above everything else. This is what makes me think I must have a hooded clitoris.'

She said it so demurely that I believed her, and assessed her as being sexually aware, but not obtrusively so.

'Why have you come to see me instead of someone else?' I asked.

'Who else is there to come to?' she pouted.

'Several,' I suggested. 'For example, Dr M.C. or Dr P.H.'

'But I saw you on television, and you sounded so sensible and so kind, I knew I must come and see you.'

I ought to have said, 'Flattery will get you nowhere!' but I did not.

'Would I be right in thinking,' I said, 'that you do have orgasm when you masturbate?'

'Oh, yes!' she replied, almost eagerly.

'How do you masturbate?'

'Well,' she said, without hesitating, 'sometimes I squeeze my legs together, sometimes I straddle the edge of the bath – which I have already made slippery with soap – and move myself backwards and forwards along it until I come, and sometimes I rub my clitoris with my finger.'

'Have you tried to look at your clitoris in a mirror?'

'I'm afraid it's never occurred to me,' she smiled innocently.

'When you stimulate your clitoris, or your partner stimulates it for you, with a finger, how long does it take you to climax – on average?'

'I've never timed myself. Naturally, it depends on how aroused I'm feeling before I begin . . .'

'Do you ever deliberately masturbate yourself with a finger when you're *not* feeling turned on?' I interrupted.

'You mean, just for something to do?'

'That's right,' I agreed. 'Or you're feeling edgy or can't sleep?'

'Yes, I do sometimes. Is that wrong?'

'Of course not. But how long does it take you to climax then – just a rough approximation?'

'Sometimes it seems like for ever, but on average – 20 minutes.'

As I made my notes, this answer seemed to indicate that there might be some condition present which was preventing the clitoral nerves from being directly stimulated.

I asked her to describe the technique she used when she masturbated manually.

'Well,' she said, appearing slightly embarrassed. 'I can feel the whole length of my clitoris under the skin, and I run my fingertip up and down one side.'

'Which side?'

She paused to consider. Then she said, 'The left side.'

'Don't you ever just rub the tip?' I asked.

Again she paused.

'No, no, I don't,' she replied.

'Doesn't your partner ever rub the tip?'

'I always ask them to rub gently up and down the side, like I do.'

'But when they go down on you, don't they stimulate the head?'

She sat up and looked at me sharply.

'I don't go in for oral sex, Dr Chartham!' she exclaimed. 'I really don't think it's nice, do you?'

'I'm afraid I do,' I told her.

Right up to this point, there had been no sign in her demeanour or in the way that she answered my questions to give me a hint that she might be acting.

'Just one more question – have you really never *once* come off during intercourse?' I persisted.

'Not once!' she answered firmly, so firmly that I believed her.

'Right!' I said, putting down my pen and standing up. 'I won't be a moment. While I'm gone, would you take off your skirt and panties . . .'

'I'm wearing tights,' she smiled.

'All right,' I smiled back. 'Take off your skirt and your tights and lie down on the couch. I'll be back in a couple of minutes.'

'I went into the bathroom to see through the two-way mirror how George was getting on with a patient for whom he was providing practical therapy. All seemed to be going well, so after watching for a couple of minutes, I went back to my consulting-room.

Now I had my first surprise.

Mrs X had not only removed her skirt and tights, but

every other garment as well, and was lying on the couch stark naked.

As I went to switch on the examination-light, I protested mildly: 'Mrs X, I said just your skirt and tights – not everything!'

'I'm wearing so little else,' she smiled. 'I thought it would be just as easy to take off everything.'

And I did notice that her breasts were rock-firm, standing up even when she lay on her back, and needed no bra; and that her belly was flat and iron-firm, needing no girdle.

I switched on the light. In retrospect, I now realise that nothing that had gone before had been as it seemed, for when I looked down at Mrs X's pubic area, my left hand already reaching out, I saw that her sex-lips were so swollen that she must have been highly sexually roused for some time. Even then, I did not sense that anything was untoward. But a moment later, when I parted her sex-lips, I did; for, looking up at me was not an average-sized clitoral head about the size of a largish *petit-pois*, but a miniature penis – completely unhooded.

I do not usually 'lose my cool' easily, but on this occasion I was immediately so angry that I felt like striking Mrs X. I opened my mouth to reprimand her, but before any word could pass my lips, she had seized me in a judo-hold, got off the couch and had me on the floor on my back, naked from the waist down.

I did pass through a course of 'unarmed' combat during World War II, in preparation for my Resistance mission, and even now at 70, can throw an attacker over my head. But on the floor of my consulting-room with Mrs X, every movement I made she countered, and caused me such pain that in a couple of minutes she had rendered me immobile.

Having got me on the floor on my back with my lower half naked, she straddled me, holding my thighs together in the tight vice of her own thighs, and her left hand locked about my left wrist. At my slightest attempt to struggle free, a vast wave of pain swept through my neck and chest, and down into my belly. After two or three tries, I realised that I really was her prisoner.

'Listen, dear doctor,' she said. 'I desperately want to make love with you. Are we going to do it comfortably, or am I going to force you, as they say in the Bible?'

'Mrs X,' I replied, 'I have made it an unbreakable rule never to become sexually involved with my patients. You have lied to me from the moment you first wrote to me, and from the first word you have spoken to me this afternoon.'

'True,' she smiled, 'but I adhere to the Jesuit doctrine that the end justifies the means.'

'You know, of course,' I told her smugly, 'that if I refuse to co-operate, there is nothing you can do to make me? You may think that you can give me an erection by twisting my arm, but I don't happen to be a masochist.'

Until this afternoon I had firmly believed that it was impossible for a woman to rape a man. Such is the control of the brain over the erection mechanism that if a man finds himself in a non-congenial sexual situation, he can prevent himself from having an erection by mentally refusing to have one, and unless he has an erection a woman cannot rape him.

But now I am not so sure!

In fact, I am so unsure that when I was asked to give evidence for the defence in a case in which a very religious young man complained that a woman and her lover had stripped him naked, tied him to a bed and the woman had repeatedly raped him, I refused. Had I not had the experience I am describing, I would gladly have been a witness on the woman's behalf on the grounds I have just stated – that a man resisting sexual stimulation cannot be induced to have the erection which only makes it possible to rape him. I still believe this to be true, but what I am not sure about is whether all men *can* always resist stimulation to erection.

I began by not wanting to have intercourse with Mrs X and was determined not to do so even when she had me locked in her vice on my back on the floor with her eager vagina only a few inches from my penis.

She smiled down at me saying, 'We shall see, doctor!' putting out her hand to fondle my penis and scrotum. Then, 'Can't I make one last plea to make love comfortably?'

I shook my head.

But I had to admit to myself that her hand caressing my genitals was a skilful one. I was determined to resist, however, and I was so successful that I noticed a wave of frustration pass over her features, which pleased me.

After a few more minutes of fruitless fondling without result, still keeping my left wrist in the grip of steel, she worked her thighs down until they gripped me just below my knees. She told me afterwards that, besides judo, she was a very keen yoga enthusiast, but at the time I was amazed when, transforming her torso into a swan's neck, she brought her mouth down to my penis.

This taught me the lesson of, in future, taking female moralistic claims with a very large grain of salt. She had been indignant when I had quizzed her about oral sex, and here she was, doing it to me.

She was not to know, of course, that after coupling itself – in other words, penis–vagina contact – I find oral sex the most exciting and the most satisfying of all sexual caresses. Added to this, she was one of the most expert fellatrices I have ever encountered. (Women, on the whole, lack the fellation skills of men.)

I think, too, that I was on the verge of needing what Kinsey quaintly calls an 'outlet' (orgasm) because, as I felt my penis begin to swell and become rigid, I had a great desire to surrender and let her have her will of me.

I told her so.

She smiled triumphantly.

'Let me take off my tunic,' I suggested. 'I feel such a fool with just the bottom half of me naked. But I warn you, I'm not going to lift a finger to help you. You're in charge – so do your best.'

And what a best it was! She was fantastic!

As I have said, until this incident, I had believed that it should be possible for any male deliberately to refuse to respond to direct stimulation, by willing himself not to do so. But I wonder how many men have the complete strength of will to deny an attractive woman's desires?

I should be interested to know what my readers think.

2 Trapped!

BEFORE WE decided to go and live in Malta for a few years, my wife and I lived in a village in Sussex, about 95 kilometres from the capital, and within a few kilometres of a mainline station which allowed me to go by train to the clinic in one-and-a-quarter hours. It was far less tiring than motoring and, besides, overcame the great difficulty of finding a parking-space once I had arrived.

The house had begun as a small four-roomed cottage built of brick which my wife, L, had bought before I married her. She had also built on to it a cedar-clad sitting-room-cum-studio – she is an artist. The house stood on a low hill-top, which gave us a view stretching for about 50 kilometres over the beautiful rolling countryside. It was a superb situation, but when I moved in, it quickly became obvious that there was not going to be enough space for me to work there on the three days a week that I did not go to London.

Fortunately, about a hectare of land surrounded the house, which made it possible for me to build a large cedar-clad study for myself adjoining the sitting-room-studio. Leading from our bedroom, I had a sauna bath installed at the same time, because I find that heat is one of the best palliatives for my arthritis, from which I have suffered since the end of the war.

A little later we built a fine studio for L on to the end of my study. Because domestic help was becoming more and more difficult to find, L had found that polishing the parquet floors was time-consuming, so we had carpets laid everywhere. Then, of course, L was afraid that she would spill paint on the carpet of that part of the sitting-room where she painted – hence the studio, where she could make as much mess as she liked.

We had scarcely finished this work, and I had sworn

never again to become involved with builders, when my doctor suggested that I ought to take more exercise than I did. My work, both at the clinic and at home, entailed my sitting for many hours at a time, and as I grew into late middle age, I started putting on weight.

As a young man I had been quite active, playing hockey and rugby, rowing, hunting (on horseback) and climbing mountains. My favourite sport since the age of five, however, has always been swimming.

The local swimming bath was very old-fashioned and unattractive and, I thought, not so hygienic as it should have been, and I thought of joining the Royal Automobile Club in London, which has a beautiful pool, and go swimming there for half an hour before going home on the days I went to the clinic. However, I wasn't very happy with this idea, because four or five hours counselling men and women with sex problems and treating them is very tiring mentally – and saps one physically – and I felt that to swim at the end of such a day would not be very wise.

One evening, while we were discussing what to do over drinks before dinner, the doorbell rang. L went to answer it, and came back with a stranger whom she introduced as Major Wales, who presented his card which declared him to be the representative of the Waterglade Swimming Pool Company. He wondered if we would be interested in having a swimming pool of our very own. If we placed an order with him within a fortnight, he could give us a reduction of £1200 off the actual price, and install it for free.

After talking it over for a day or two, we agreed to have one of Major Wales's swimming pools – which was to be heated – and, the British climate being what it is, in order to get the most out of it, we decided to have it, too, clad in cedar, so that we could swim in it all the year round.

It was sited at the back of L's studio, and it was fantastic to slip out of bed about half-past six in the morning, and after having set some coffee filtering, to run naked through the dining-room, sitting-room, study and studio, swim a kilometre and come back glowing and full of vitality to a

cup of coffee. Before dinner – when L usually joined me – I swam another kilometre.

(To my mind, there is nothing so sensually exciting as swimming naked. Making love in a swimming-pool, too, is much more of an experience than in the biggest of baths – there is so much more room.)

On the day of the episode which I wish to relate, I had had five difficult clients. I say 'difficult' clients because, though they presented straightforward cases of dysfunction, there was something about each one which, nevertheless, made the case appear 'difficult'. I am sure that my professional colleagues will agree with me that some days everything falls into place and one wonders why both oneself and the client have spent an hour smoothing out some sexual fear, giving reassurance, listening to a story which must be told, but the teller has no one he/she dares confide in; while on other days, although there is an easy solution, it is only with difficulty that one can convince the client of it.

I must confess that one of the cases on this day was *not* easy. It involved a girl who greatly desired to make love, but believed that every penis would cause her great pain. We had been working together for several weeks, but progress was slow, and today we had made no progress at all.

Well, at the end of the day I was very weary. To add to my misery, it was raining lightly as I waited at the taxi rank for a taxi to take me to Charing Cross. By the time my train had reached the halfway point of the journey, the rain was beating against the carriage windows and there were intermittent flashes of lightning and claps of thunder.

I got down from the train and, by the time I had crossed the few steps to my car which I had parked in the station yard, even my raincoat was wet through, and the deluge of rain reduced vision to a couple of metres, making my journey twice as long. When I did arrive, I was not only even more tired and very wet, but bad-tempered as well.

L had introduced a very pleasant custom of meeting me at the door when I returned from London, with a glass of

whisky in her hand. This evening I needed it more than ever. We embraced, she took my wet raincoat and I took the glass and went straight to our bedroom, where I stripped off my wet and crumpled clothes, took a sip of the inwardly warming whisky and ran naked through the house to the swimming pool.

L had said that she would not join me because she was cooking one of her specialities, a great favourite of mine – casserole of pigeon with red cabbage and apple, and several other accessories. It was a great pity, as it turned out, because I was soon to discover that I 'needed' her.

Ever since I can remember, when I have been playing a hard game, or become extra weary at work, and have got into a steaming bath to ease aching limbs, almost immediately I have become randy, and more than usually so.

Our pool wasn't exactly a hot bath, though it did steam, the water temperature being kept at 27°C. This evening I had swum only a couple of lengths when I became aware that the sensuous movement of the water over my body was sexually exciting me. By the time I had finished another length of the pool I had a raging erection. If only L had been with me! But she wasn't, and there was no way of calling her.

I finished my kilometre with my penis cleaving the water beneath me like a harpoon or, if I turned on to my back, resembling a gun on a half-surfaced submarine's deck. It was still as vigorously upright when I climbed out and finished drying myself.

I ran along to the kitchen to show L, but when she saw it, she said, 'Darling, impossible! Dinner's almost ready and I can't leave it. Go and put on your kaftan, get yourself another whisky and look at the TV news. That will take your mind off it.'

I know L well enough to realise that it is no use arguing with her when she is cooking. So I did as she said, and by the time she called me to the table, my erection had half-subsided, but not enough for L not to see it pushing out my kaftan as I walked and remark, 'Poor old chap! He does want it badly!'

After dinner, we sat and watched TV, but I was almost distracted from the play by the truly intensely voluptuous sensations provoked by my own randiness which had returned in full, and the response L was making to it. While we were thus pleasurably engaged, the telephone rang.

'Don't answer it!' I whispered to L, biting the lobe of one of her ears lightly.

'But it may be urgent . . . one of the children.' It was her stock reply to my resistance to the telephone. I hate the damned instrument.

'If it's urgent, they'll ring again soon,' I said as usual.

'All right,' she said.

But part of the spell was broken, and though I was still enjoying it and was almost coming off, I didn't prevent her from getting off me and answering the telephone when it rang again five minutes later.

She came back from the study a couple of minutes later saying, 'It's Robin T. He says he's stuck and it's very urgent!'

'Stuck!' I exclaimed. 'Where's he stuck?'

'He didn't say,' she smiled. 'But I can think of one place.'

'Don't be silly,' I said. 'That rarely happens.'

I went to the study with my unsatisfied penis feeling definitely thwarted. Nevertheless, I knew that, if Robin was in difficulty and wanted my help, he really did need my help.

Robin was, I should explain, 32, a bachelor and lived in a luxury apartment in a seaside resort some 30 kilometres distant. He and I had been very close friends for a time before I married L.

I picked up the phone. 'Hello, Robin,' I said. 'You are an inconsiderate sod. I'll explain why later. L tells me you're stuck and that it's urgent. Where the hell are you and how are you stuck?'

'I'm at home,' he said, 'and I'm stuck in my lovely lady.'

'I don't believe it!' I said.

'It's true,' he said. 'Céline, tell him it's true.'

A woman's voice said into the phone, 'It's true! Please come and unstick us.'

'How long have you been like this?' I asked Robin.

'Nearly an hour!'

'Oh God!' I exclaimed. 'Why didn't you phone me before?'

'We thought she or I would relax and it would be all right. Can you be quick? It's beginning to hurt like hell.'

'I'll be with you in half an hour.'

The predicament in which Robin and his girl-friend found themselves was not only rare, fortunately, but could be painful for Robin, and dangerous if he were not rescued soon. (In all my years of experience, I have encountered only one other case, though I know some colleagues who have had experience of a few cases, while others maintain it is a sexual myth.)

What had happened was that Céline had been afflicted by a spasm of the sphincter muscle of her vagina entrance – a condition called *vaginismus* – which had caused the muscle to close tightly and clamp itself round Robin's penis so that he could not withdraw.

Although vaginismus is a not uncommon reaction in psychosexually frightened women – by closing the vagina they prevent the penis from entering – cases of *penis captivus* seldom arise. But when one does, unless treatment is quickly obtained, it usually is very painful for the man, and it can also be dangerous because, in severe cases, circulation of the blood through the penis may be affected and this can lead to subsequent circulatory problems, giving rise, in some cases, to long periods of impotence.

'I'm on my way,' I reassured Robin and, hanging up the telephone, hurried through the bedroom, where I pulled on some clothes. I briefly explained to L what had happened, and then ran back to the study and got a phial of diazepam in solution, a couple of disposable hypodermic needles and one or two other odds and ends which I thought I might need.

As I was leaving the study, it suddenly struck me that Robin would not be able to let me into his apartment. I wondered whether there was still a night porter who could let me in with his pass-key.

Then I had a brain-wave. I never throw away a key, and in a drawer of my desk there must be three dozen or more odd keys fitting I don't know what. I'd had a key to Robin's apartment when he and I had been 'best friends', and couldn't recall having given it back to him. It was a very distinctive key, because it shone like gold. I pushed about in the heap in the drawer, and there, hidden at the bottom, it was.

Fortunately it had stopped raining heavily, though it had not stopped altogether, and to add to my luck, there was little traffic going down to the coast, although quite a lot coming the opposite way. It took me just 30 minutes from the time Robin had telephoned to reach his apartment.

It was as well that I had found the key, because there had been no porters at the apartments for a couple of years. I would have had to call out the resident caretaker, and by the time I had convinced him that I had to get to Robin as quickly as possible, precious time would have been lost. Not only that, tongues would have wagged.

To say the least, it is an embarrassing situation for both victims to find themselves in.

I flung off my coat in the hall, and hurried to the bedroom. They had been coupling in the missionary position, and Robin, who was moaning quietly with pain, was almost crushing the life out of Céline with his weight, although he was doing his best not to.

As I took off my jacket and rolled up my shirt sleeves, I said, 'I want you to roll over so that Céline is on top. I'm just going to wash my hands.'

But when I came back from the bathroom, they were still as they had been.

'I must have Céline on top, because I can't get at the vital spot as you are now,' I insisted. I wanted to inject the diazepam as near as possible to the mid-point of Céline's perineum – the ridge between the anus and the lower vagina edge in women, and the anus and high up behind the scrotum in men.

To be brief, with my help they were able to roll over. Then, of course, we had to manoeuvre Robin's legs

together so that Cèline could spread her legs on either side of him. In that position, her perineum was more accessible to me.

I filled the hypodermic with the solution of diazepam which, I believed, would relax the vaginal muscle more quickly than if I had given her any other tranquilliser or even diazepam by mouth. I cleaned her perineum and anus with surgical spirit, located the spot I was aiming for, and stuck the needle in, discharged and withdrew it.

'Had you come off before this happened?' I asked Robin.

'No,' he said. 'I wasn't far off, but I hadn't come.'

'I had a couple of times,' Céline said.

'I'm more interested in Robin at the moment.' I think I spoke a little too sharply, because when I asked Robin if he thought he still had an erection, and he said he couldn't tell, her voice trembled as she asked, 'May I speak, please?'

'Of course!' I said, more kindly.

'Erect or not,' she said, 'he feels bloody big to me.'

Having had so little experience of the trapped penis, I had not 'read up' on it. I knew that a relaxing agent was necessary and I had been experimenting in therapy for premature ejaculation with diazepam in solution with some success. But what I did not know was whether the penis was more likely to be damaged if trapped erect or while it was subsiding after orgasm.

While waiting for the diazepam to take effect, I asked Céline if this had ever happened to her before, and she said no.

'What happened this time?' I asked.

'Céline and I have only known one another a week,' Robin said, 'and this is the first time we've had it off. I had booked a table at La Tavernetta, and Céline came to call for me. We had a drink, then one thing led to another and we decided to go to bed and have dinner afterwards. I had hoped that she would agree to come back for the night with me.'

'I would have, too,' she said. 'Of course you wouldn't know, doctor, but he's one of the best and most sexy men at turning a girl on that I've ever met.'

Robin winked at me, and I winked back.

'Well,' he continued, 'the time came for me to go in her, and she was making appreciative noises and I was holding back for as long as I could, though I would not have been able to much longer, when suddenly the telephone rang.'

'It gave me such a fright, doctor,' Céline said, 'because I hadn't seen a telephone in the room. How was I to know that it was hidden away in that bedside cupboard?'

'Of course you weren't!' I commiserated – on several occasions I have sent that instrument to damnation for ringing at the wrong moment. 'Why the hell, Robin, didn't you take the damn thing off the hook when you got into bed?'

'If you'd seen Susie as I'd seen Susie,' he sang, 'you wouldn't have thought of that blasted telephone either. I was so worked up . . .'

'I understand,' I said.

'He was!' said Céline. 'It was lovely! It does a girl such a lot of good to know that she can have that sort of effect on a fellow! Now I'm teaching my grandmother to suck eggs.'

'Not at all,' I assured her.

'I know this happens to dogs,' Robin said, 'but I didn't know it can happen to humans. Of course, I've heard of couples getting stuck and having to be carted off to hospital to get unstuck, but I thought they were just bar jokes.'

'It doesn't happen very often,' I said. 'And with the wonders of modern medicine . . . Feel any easier?'

'It's not hurting now,' Robin said.

'Céline,' I said, 'raise your bottom up very slowly.' But when she tried to do so, Robin let out a slight yelp, so we had to wait a little longer.

'I wish you'd telephoned me earlier,' I said.

'I told you that we thought we'd get unstuck if we waited a few minutes,' Robin said. 'Anyway, why didn't you answer the first time I rang?'

'I'm sorry,' I laughed.

I explained. 'I thought you sounded a bit annoyed,' he managed to grin.

'You're lucky,' I said. 'L's a compulsive telephone

answerer. Try to get him out of you again, dear,' I urged again.

Very slowly she raised her haunches, and this time Robin did not yelp. So she went all the way and he came out of her with a plopping sound.

'Do you think you could pee if you went to the loo?' I asked Céline. I thought that, if she could, it would relax her completely.

'I'll try,' she said, quite unembarrassed as she climbed off the bed and ran across the room into the bathroom.

Robin's penis was not erect, but though flexible it was swollen to its erect size. The head was dark purple, the skin of the shaft darker than usual, and the visible veins and especially the great dorsal one, were swollen like varicous veins.

'God! What a sight!' Robin exclaimed. 'Is it a goner?'

'I don't think so. I hope not!' I replied sincerely. I stroked the unsightly organ lightly. 'Does that hurt?'

'No,' he said.

'Got any KY jelly?' I asked.

'I think so,' he said. 'Don't have to use it often these days.'

'Same place?' I asked. He nodded.

I opened the drawer of the bedside table above the cupboard which housed the offending telephone.

I found it and at the same time took the telephone from the cupboard and put it on the bed.

'I want to try to get the circulation in your penis working normally again, and while I'm doing it, you can phone L and say I'll be home in just over an hour full of expectations.'

So while I attended to him, he telephoned L, who wanted to speak to me, but I said I couldn't stop what I was doing and, if she was merely curious, Robin would tell her. He passed on the message and then suddenly realised what L had said. 'I damn well won't,' he said, loud enough for L to hear. Then he put the telephone down and said, 'All she wanted to say was that she loves you excitedly, and that you would know what that means.'

Céline came back.
'Successful?' I asked her.
'Yes, thank you,' she said demurely. 'Why are you doing that?'
I told her. 'Look!' I said.
'Oh, my poor darling!' she exclaimed, bending over Robin and kissing him. 'Will it be all right ever again?'
'Yes,' I said. 'I believe so.'
At the end of about half an hour, the mauled organ was back to its normal flaccid proportions, though the skin was still a rather dark grey.
I went to the bathroom and washed my hands. When I came back they were sitting silently on the edge of the bed, with Céline's arm round Robin's neck.
'Now, you two,' I said. 'This could happen again to Céline if a telephone rings while she's having it off, but not otherwise! I stress *not otherwise*. So, Céline, never go to bed with someone who has a telephone by his bedside, unless he takes it off the hook. OK?'
'OK,' she agreed.
'What I think would be best for you to do is to go and have dinner at La Tavernetta, then come back and have an orgy for two,' I said. 'If you get into any more trouble – which I'm sure you won't – don't hesitate to ring at once. But not before midnight, because I shan't be answering before then.'
'How much am I in your debt?' Robin asked.
'What's a *penis captivus* between friends?' I said.
Two days later, two cases of whisky were delivered to our home.
What I don't understand is, why was I still so randy after all that, that I practically raped L?

3 The Gentle Rapist

IF ANY sexologist, psychosexual therapist or marriage counsellor talks to you about *normal* sexual desire, *normal* sexual behaviour, *normal* sexual performance, *normal* sexual capacity or anything else *normal* related to the sexual experience, you should know at once that he or she is a charlatan. There is no such being as a *normally* sexual man or woman; we are all sexual individuals.

Similarly, if you ever make contact with the specialists I have mentioned above, and they tell you that, whatever your problem is, there is a solution, do *not* believe them. A man or woman who makes such a claim is not only a charlatan, he/she is a fool, because sooner or later you are going to discover that there are some problems to which there is no satisfactory solution.

I was 19 when I began (with official approval) to counsel younger teenagers, way back in 1929; and it is just a little short of 40 years since I took my doctorate in the psychology of sexual dysfunction. Except for four years during World War II, I have been counselling and providing therapy for sexually unhappy boys and girls, men and women, heteros and gays.

Why is it, that after all these years devoted to sex, that I make the statement I have given above? Experience!

I am not saying that the majority of cases are not capable of solution; I am saying that the experience of my consulting-room has taught me that it is not only disillusioning but dangerous to assure any patient that, if he/she pays you a fee each time he/she comes to visit you for one hour, at the end of one, five or countless sessions, the problem will have been overcome.

Quite early I discovered the truth of what I am saying, and a truth so conclusive that, for 30 years at least, I have treated each problem as a unique one that must be solved

on its merits – or, I should say, has the capability of solution, taking all the factors *individually* into consideration.

So what has all this to do with rape?

Ever since my late teens I have been inclined to the view that a woman need not be raped if she doesn't want to be raped unless the direst threats cause her extreme fear for her life, or she is unconscious. Women of quite ordinary build and strength acquire extraordinary strength in their thighs and legs when resisting undesired male sexual advances.

When I was at Cambridge and was training for rowing for my college, I was at the peak of my physical fitness and strength, unsurpassed throughout my life except when I was preparing for my mission as a secret agent during the last war. During the earlier period I had a couple of girl-friends who took great delight in teasing me sexually by refusing to let me couple with them when I wanted to.

Naturally, I did not threaten them or actually hurt them in any way, but I did wrestle with them to make them open their legs, and I was powerless. When they crossed their legs, only fear of me would have made them open them – except, of course, when they were sexually ready to do so of their own free will.

A case I had a year or two ago confirmed me in this belief, and made me a keen supporter of that clause in the recent Bill which protects the alleged rapist from being named unless he is found guilty.

Grace asked for a counselling session, and Sylvia, my receptionist, arranged one for her, showing her, at the appointed time, into my consulting-room.

She was a pretty little thing rather than lovely, and from the embarrassed nervousness she betrayed, my impression was that she was not very sexually sophisticated. I asked her to sit down and began to ask the usual background questions for my records.

She was 21 and had been married for a year to a man four years older, who had a very good job as the manager of a large house-furnishing store. She herself was employed as a

personal assistant to the director of a firm of insurance brokers.

Grace and her husband owned their house on a mortgage, and had decided not to have children for a time. Was she on the Pill? No! The doctors had advised her not to be. So what contraceptive did they use? The diaphragm cap.

'How do you find it?' I asked. I was interested, because in my young days, the Pill had not been discovered and before I had my vasectomy – in 1939, the third or fourth man in Europe to do so – we had used the diaphragm cap.

'To begin with,' Grace told me, 'it was a bit of a nuisance, since you never know when you are going to make love, do you? I now put it in every night when we go to bed, as a matter of routine. If we make love, I leave it in all day, until I come home; if we don't make love, I take it out before going to the office. The only small chore is cleaning it.'

'And you feel perfectly safe using it?' I asked.

'I've never thought about it. I've just taken it for granted. What do you think?'

'It never let my wife and I down over five years,' I told her.

By this time she was relaxing, and had stopped uncrossing and recrossing her legs and fiddling with her gloves. She was actually smiling, too.

I now felt I could ask her: 'Did you and your husband have it away before you married?'

She shook her head. 'No! Pat is a bit old-fashioned. His mum is rather a gorgon and was always at him about behaving so-called morally.'

I was beginning to revise my first assessment of her, and felt emboldened to ask the following questions.

'Were you a virgin before you married Pat? I don't mean to be rude or inquisitive,' I said, 'but it does help to know how sexually experienced you are.'

'I had sex twice before I met Pat,' she said, after a small hesitation.

'Did you enjoy it?' I asked.

'One, yes . . . The other, nothing happened.'

'What do you mean by "nothing happened"?'

'I wasn't satisfied.'

'Right,' I said. 'What are your sexual relations with your husband like?'

She paused for quite a time before she answered. Eventually she said, 'I don't quite know what to say without sounding disloyal to Pat.'

'My dear,' I said. 'You've asked me to have a chat with you. It's going to cost you quite a lot of money. If you can't be absolutely frank with me, you're wasting your money and my time. In this room, every word uttered is confidential, and I can't really help unless you forget about so-called loyalty. Do you understand? And don't forget – I've probably heard everything there is to hear about sexual relationships between husbands and wives, or anybody else for that matter! If you want my help, be utterly frank! No one else will know, but me.'

'I'm sorry,' she said. 'I'm being stupid. But, you see – I've been raped.'

At once I was very sympathetic, whether or not my sympathy was misplaced.

'Why didn't you say so at once?' I asked quietly.

'Because the whole business seems to be getting out of control.'

I knew she could not mean that, but it disclosed her state of mind to me.

'OK,' I said, 'but first answer my question about your sexual relationship with Pat.'

Again she was silent for a few seconds. Then she said, 'I would like to explain something . . .'

'Anything!' I tried to encourage her.

'I love Pat very much. He's kind and he's gorgeous to look at, but sexually he doesn't satisfy me really. On the other hand, I would never consider parting from him just on that account. Apart from sex, I have no complaints.'

'Good,' I said. 'Have you any specific sexual complaint against him?'

'Well, I've read one or two books which describe other positions besides the man lying on top of the woman. I

would like to try me on top of him, but he says it's not the right way.'

'You're saying that he's not very adventurous?'

'Well, yes! But there is another reason why I'd like to try it some other way.'

'Tell me.'

'He's never given me a climax while he's inside me. I've never come near to a climax any time we've made love. I know it's not my fault, because I can do it for myself any time I want to – you know.'

'So you would like me to see him?' I suggested.

She seemed startled.

'Oh no!' she exclaimed. 'I would really like him not to know I've been to see you.'

'Then why have you come to see me?' I asked again.

'I told you – I've been raped and I feel awfully bad about what I have done,' she said seriously.

I waited quietly, expecting her to recount the usual story of attack, fear and degradation.

'You'll think I'm a funny person,' she said, smiling faintly.

'Well, suppose you tell me what happened, and I'll tell you whether or not I think you're funny,' I encouraged her.

She paused and then began. 'The window-cleaner comes round once a month. My neighbour kindly pays him and I repay her. He only does the outsides of the windows. I've only seen him once or twice, but he's about Pat's age, quite good-looking, nicely spoken and polite. A little shy, even.

'I had one or two days' leave from the office due to me and I decided to take a day off and do some shopping in London for some things I needed and couldn't get locally. I had arranged to meet a friend in Oxford Street for lunch, and after lunch we'd go shopping, so I was not in any particular hurry after I'd got Pat his breakfast and seen him off. I was going to have an unhurried bath and take a mid-morning train.

'I was just going to run the bath when I heard the windows being cleaned . . . There is a kind of skylight on the landing which Pat can't reach using our steps. It was

very dirty inside, and I had been hoping I would catch the window cleaner one day soon, and ask him to come in with his ladder and clean it for me. So I went to the door and spoke to him.'

'How were you dressed?' I asked, now beginning to get the drift.

'In a long, silk, genuine Japanese kimono, which reaches down to the floor. It was a wedding present from one of my uncles who's a captain in the merchant navy.'

'Anything else?' I asked.

'Slippers. Why?'

'Never mind for the moment. Go on!'

'I asked him if he could clean the window, and he said he would come and have a look at it. So I took him up to the landing, and he said he could reach it on his short ladder, but he wouldn't be able to clean the outside without unscrewing the hinges. I said it didn't matter about the outside, and he said it was up to me, but there wasn't much point in cleaning the inside, with the outside as dirty as it was.

'I asked him how long it would take to unscrew the hinges and he said he could finish the job in about ten minutes and it would cost me 40 pence extra. I thought it was worth it, so I asked him to do it. So he fetched his ladder, bucket, chamois and his tools.'

She paused and began to blush. Quickly she said, 'I don't think you are going to believe me when I tell you that the thought never crossed my mind at the time that I was being provocative. But I swear . . .'

'Grace, I do believe you,' I assured her.

'Honestly?' she asked.

'Honestly!' I said. 'Go on.'

'I followed him upstairs, and said to him, "When you've finished, I'll be in here," and pointed to the door of our bedroom. "Just call out and I'll pay you." I could hear him working out on the landing as I took the varnish off my nails.

'I hadn't fixed my nails properly for quite a time, because I was always in a hurry, and unless they were very badly

chipped, I just painted over them . . . Anyhow, just as I was finishing getting the old varnish completely off, I *thought* I heard a little tap on the door. Without thinking, I called out, "Come in." Do you still believe me?'

'Yes,' I said, and I did because it is a reflex action to call out 'come in' when you hear a knock on your door.

'Thank God!' she said. 'I saw him in my dressing-table mirror coming over to me, a rather strange look in his eyes which frightened me a little bit; at least, enough to stop me from moving.

'He came up to me and stood behind me. Then, gently pulling the front of my kimono apart, he put his hands over my breasts, and ran his tongue up and down the nape of my neck. I remember his words exactly.

' "You are so lovely," he said. "Let me make love to you." '

'He didn't threaten?' I asked.

'No,' she said.

'So?'

'You must think me depraved.'

'Not yet,' I told her, 'but don't keep me in suspense!'

'His touch had turned me on, as I don't remember having been turned on before. Perhaps the fact that Pat hadn't made love to me the previous evening had something to do with it – but I'm not making excuses.'

'Did you agree to make love with him?' I asked.

'I didn't speak! But on the other hand, I didn't resist.'

'What happened?'

'He must have taken my silence for consent, because before I had realised what was happening, he was naked and so was I, and he was lifting me on to the bed.'

'And you weren't resisting at all?'

'No! He was so gentle and kind, and I was in a kind of *conscious* trance. To be frank, his foreplay technique was fantastic. He did to me things which I don't think Pat would do even if he knew about them. I was, as they say, "putty" – very compliant putty – "in his hands".'

'Did you respond with foreplay on him?'

'No, I didn't touch him, but I saw his penis . . .'

'And?'

'. . . it was beautiful! Pat's is slightly arched and the head is not in proportion with the shaft. *His* was absolutely straight, so dominating, so . . . so . . .'

'So, what happened?'

'I was nearly coming when he eventually came into me. He had judged it to the second. Thinking it over since, I believe that the reason I don't come off with Pat is that he doesn't play with me long enough.'

'It could be,' I said.

'I didn't have to help him in, like I do Pat, and he *filled* me, and it was lovely! . . . To be brief, I didn't come off just once, but twice before he came.'

'And afterwards?'

'I was vaguely aware of losing him, and then being on my own, and with so pleasant a sensation of being satisfied. I just lay there, purring like a cat until . . .

'I remembered I had not had my cap in. I told you that when we don't make love, I take the cap out when I get up. The thought that I might become pregnant made me feel totally numb. Do you realise, Dr Chartham, that I have only come off three times with a penis inside me, and two of those times – *twice*,' she almost shouted, 'with him, and it all might be spoiled because he could have made me pregnant.

'I just lay there wondering what to do. I couldn't think of anything, until it struck me that I could "forget" to put my cap in on a night when Pat made love to me . . . Aren't I dreadful?'

'I don't think so,' I told her. 'After all, you were in a big dilemma.'

'Well, I stirred myself at last and went into the bathroom and began to draw a bath. Just as I was going to get into it, the front-door bell rang. Feeling a bit nervous, I went down to answer it. Betty, my neighbour, was there.

'She looked a bit startled. I had forgotten to put my kimono on and was stark naked. "Grace, dear! Has something happened? Where's Alfred?" she asked.

' "Who's Alfred?" I asked.

'"The window-cleaner," she said. "I saw him cleaning your windows but he hasn't been to me. Why not?"

'I began to feel faint, and swayed against the wall by the door. "Are you all right, Grace?" she asked. I couldn't speak. She came in and shut the door. "Has something happened?" she asked, and I heard myself saying, "He raped me."'

Grace did not know quite what happened next, except a kind of swamping by well-meaning friends, followed by the arrival of the police.

'The most awful part was being examined by the police-surgeon, who later gave evidence that he had found semen in my vagina,' Grace told me.

'So what happened?' I asked.

'If only the dear fellow had not panicked and fled, I would have said nothing, and if I had got pregnant I would have told Pat that I had forgotten my cap.'

'But you said to your neighbour, "He raped me,"' I reminded her.

'I hadn't expected him to run away. He must have known that I wouldn't have complained. Then Betty ringing the bell knocked me off balance, and I got confused.'

'I can understand that,' I told her. 'But what do you want me to do?'

'I don't know,' she said.

'You do,' I said. 'You need me to ease your conscience. You enjoyed sex with Alfred more than you do with your husband. There's no difficulty there. You must educate your husband to satisfy you. Insist on it!'

'It's not so simple as that, doctor,' she said.

'Why not?' I asked.

'They caught him and brought him to trial,' she said.

'Naturally,' I told her.

'But this is what is so awful. He pleaded guilty so that I should not have to give evidence. He was sentenced to eighteen months' imprisonment.'

There was a long pause.

'Your dilemma is an unusual one,' I said eventually. 'What you want to know is what you can do to straighten

out your conscience. If you had been brave enough to tell the truth, you would have lost your husband, probably.'

'Certainly if I had told him that being raped was much more enjoyable than making love with him.'

'It is difficult, isn't it?' I commented.

I told her that I had never had a case like this, and that I would have to think about it. I would write to her.

When I did eventually write to her, I played for time.

'Was she pregnant?' I wanted to know.

She telephoned and left a message: no, she was not pregnant.

'Then,' I wrote again, 'the only advice I can give you is not to tell your husband the truth of what happened, and you could help the man you so much enjoyed, by sending him parcels of good things to eat.'

She had a sense of humour, because she wrote briefly, 'He "ate" me, but I will give him something which, though more ordinary, must be more tasteful.'

I am haunted by this case.

I should be most grateful to any of my readers if they would tell me what I should have advised.

The only thought I can leave with you is: Rape is not always what it seems!

4 In Need of Love

I DON'T think anyone would say that Mary is pretty, and I think, too, that many males would not find her physically attractive unless they were desperate for sex, or had feelings of sexual inadequacy, or were sexual perverts of one kind or another who could bully her into complying with their *outré* sexual desires.

Unfortunately, Mary has not got a very high IQ either, but none of these things – physical and mental – means that she is not in need of love as much as the 'Beautiful People'.

I noticed all this as she came into my consulting-room in response to an invitation to come and see me after I had received a brief letter from her that was full of despair. It didn't exactly strike me as *strange*, but, nevertheless, something out of the ordinary, that she was wearing a hat and spotless white cotton gloves, which young people of her age don't normally go in for these days.

She was carrying a plastic carrier-bag bearing the august name of Harrods. Her bulging handbag, however, was very shabby and worn.

She responded to my smile of welcome with a kind of gratitude. When I asked her to sit down, she did so sedately, crossing her legs and drawing off her gloves.

'Dr Chartham,' she said at once, 'before we begin, I must tell you that I have very little money. Perhaps I shall not be able to afford your fee. I ought to have asked in my letter what your fee would be, but I forgot until I was coming here this afternoon. I am so desperate.'

'Well,' I said, 'I'm glad you've come. Will you, please, forget all about money? Promise?'

'I promise,' she smiled nervously.

'OK then. How old are you?'

'Twenty-four.'

'Married or single.'

'Single – but I have a little boy.'

I think that I reacted to this piece of information without surprise – one schools oneself not to *appear* surprised at anything one's patients confide; indeed, I don't think that anything anyone would tell me would now surprise me – although I must admit that I was just a little inwardly surprised, in view of the description that I have given of Mary, to learn that she did have a child.

'What's your little boy's name?' I asked.

'George. He's a little devil!' she exclaimed with love.

'How old?'

'Three.'

'Do you have brothers or sisters?'

'No.'

'Are your mother and father living?'

'I've never known who my father was. My mother died when I was 20. I have uncles and aunts, but they don't seem to like me very much. They held it against me that I am illegitimate, and since I've had George, they're even more nasty. But I don't mind. One aunt said, "What do you expect? Like mother, like daughter" and none of them has a leg to stand on when it comes to being really innocent.'

'Do you have a job?' I asked.

'No, I can't get one that would pay me sufficient to have George looked after. I do some baby-sitting myself sometimes. I rely on Social Security and George's father gives me £5 a week, but if you can do something about him, I shall lose that. But I don't mind, so long as I can be out of bondage to him.' (It was only later that the real significance of her use of the sexual-jargon word 'bondage' struck me.)

'Can you give me a brief idea of your experience?' I asked. 'Feel free to tell me anything, in the words you are used to.'

There was a considerable pause, during which she looked down at her hands. Then she looked at me and said, 'Do you know, I think I can tell you everything.'

'All right,' I said. 'Let's start.'

'I began late. I was 16 when I had my first period,' she said.

'If I say "masturbate" or "bring yourself off", do you know what I mean?' I asked.

'Yes, I know what you mean,' she smiled, 'but I call it pleasuring myself.'

'A good word,' I smiled back at her. 'When did you first pleasure yourself?'

'After I had begun my periods. Probably 17. I can remember the first time very well. I had this funny tense kind of feeling between my legs and I just had to finger my – cunt.'

She looked at me as if to gauge my reaction to her use of the word.

'"Cunt" is a very good word,' I said. 'Nothing shameful about it.'

She giggled quietly, then she said, 'What a relief! Now I can talk to you as real woman-to-man.'

This surprised me and I wondered if her IQ was as low as I had assessed it. Perhaps she wasn't so innocent after all.

Before I could ask her my next question, she said, 'When I first pleasured myself, it was fantastic. It opened up a whole new world to me.'

'Tell me,' I said, 'after you had your first orgasm – the first time you came off – what was it like?'

'I just said – it took me into another world, Dr Chartham. It was such a beautiful feeling, I just kept on doing it.'

'And you were happy?'

'You are not going to be like all the rest of them,' she said, 'wanting to know what it felt like second by second?'

'Who are all the others?'

'All the girls I ever talk to about it.'

I would have liked to have known what it felt like to her, but realised that I would lose her trust if I probed too deeply. 'No,' I assured her. 'When did you have your first fuck?'

'When I was 20. It wasn't very good, because the boy came before I did, and didn't do anything to help me. But I liked the feel of him inside me, so when another boy asked

me if we could do it a few months later, I said yes. It was better this time, because he took me to his room and we did it properly in bed without any clothes on. The first time had been on Hampstead Heath behind a bush.'

'Did you come off the second time?'

'Yes. But he had pleasured me until I was nearly coming before he came into me. Yes, I liked it, and I liked it each time we did it.'

'Which was how often?' I asked.

'About once a week for three or four months. David was a nice, kind boy, not quite as old as me, but he had a lovely cock, really beautiful to look at whether it was soft or stiff. He had been circumcised. He showed me how to play with it and suck it. He used to go down on me, too. I was just beginning to get really fond of him, when he decided to join the merchant navy and went away and I've never seen him again.'

If she was telling me the truth, then my first reactions to her looks had to be revised. It is well known that there are women who are attracted to a man because of his physical ugliness, so maybe there are men who are attracted to plain women. But I have yet to meet them, so perhaps these partners of Mary, though apparently sexually experienced, had some feelings of inadequacy. It was a pity I could not question them.

'About a year after he had gone,' she went on, 'I met Philip. Philip was nearly 30, and I always had the feeling that he was married. I asked him once if he was, but he said no, and got quite angry.'

'And there wasn't anyone between David and Philip?' I asked.

'No,' she said. 'I don't go out looking for men. They've got to make the first move. Mind you, I've often been tempted to make up to a man I like the look of, because I've been terribly lonely, and it's really lovely to be in a man's arms, and to have his cock in you and you make him happy, but somehow I've never had the courage to say to a boy, "Wouldn't you like to fuck me?" so I never have.'

'Tell me about Philip,' I said.

'He was a strange man. He didn't say much, but he was kind and I think he loved me in a mild kind of way. Mum had died by the time I met him. After she died, I went to live with an uncle and aunt but they were so tight-lipped, I wasn't happy with them. I had a job then, as a shop assistant at a confectioner's. When I first met Philip, I had just got myself a room, and as he didn't seem to have anywhere to go, I took him there.'

'How did you meet Philip?'

'In a pub one Saturday night. There was another girl in the shop with me, and she suggested we should go to this pub together. Philip was there with another chap, and they came over to our table and started chatting us up. They bought us drinks and seemed kind, and we had a good laugh, and then Philip's friend went off with my friend and they didn't come back. Philip and I went on chatting and we had more drinks, and then he took my hand under the table and put it between his legs and there was a huge bulge, which made me start to come on.

'I suppose I ought to have taken my hand away, but instead I thought how nice it would be to have him in bed with me, but I didn't suggest it. I just squeezed his cock, and he said, "Would you like to give John Thomas a home?"

'I nodded, and he said, "Let's go out to the car, then," and I said, "I've got a room quite near here. Let's go there." Then I had the shock of my life, because he said, "How much do you ask, then?" It took me a couple of minutes to understand what he meant, and when I did, I felt angry, and then I thought, well, no sense in being angry because it feels interesting, so I said, "I do it for love," and he said, "You're a great girl," and squeezed my thigh and said, "Let's go."

'I haven't seen many cocks, mind you, but his was huge. Not long, but thick. Almost as thick as my wrist, and I'm not exaggerating. He had a beautiful body, too, strong and big muscles, but he was so gentle. When I saw that lovely cock, I just had to go down on it, and do you know, Dr Chartham, it was the first time anyone had gone down on him, and I sent him wild. It made me very proud that I could

do that for a man. But I had my reward, because when he came in me, he really stretched me and I came off twice before he came. I could feel this huge cock jerking about inside me when he came, and that made me come a third time.

'He left me about two in the morning, which made me suspect that he might be married, because next day was Sunday, and he could have stayed all day.'

'Are you on the Pill?' I asked her.

She shook her head. 'I don't like the idea of it,' she said.

'I suppose your partners used french letters?' I asked.

'The first boy didn't David, but Philip did after the first time. We had a lot of lovely Saturday nights together. But he always left between two and three on Sunday morning.'

'What happened to him?' I asked.

'He just didn't turn up one Saturday evening, and I've never seen him again. I was very upset about losing Philip.'

'So then?'

'After a few months George's father came into my life, as the romantic novelists would say. It's about him that I've come to see you.'

'OK,' I said. 'Go on.'

'He's a Pakistani. He was training to be a dentist when I met him in a disco. He was quite different from Philip – I mean, he was very dark-skinned, covered in long black hair. He was very skinny, almost a skeleton, and although his cock was half as long again as Philip's, it wasn't much thicker than your thumb. I didn't know there could be so many variations.'

'I've never seen two exactly the same,' I smiled.

'How many have you seen?' she asked.

'Hundreds,' I told her.

'Of course,' she said. 'You've done your survey.'

'Tell me more,' I said.

'He always came too soon at first, but then he got better, and he also got very greedy. He was selfish, too. He wouldn't help me off if I didn't come, but he could do things to me with that slender rod of his that felt nice. Still, I never became really fond of him.

'He used to come round nearly every evening, and that I liked, because I wasn't lonely any more, and I thought that perhaps Pakistanis just don't show their feelings very much. Sometimes he'd take me to a Wimpy bar, but never anywhere more grand. He liked me to cook for him in my room. Sometimes he bought some food or a bottle of wine, but not *very* often. Then all of a sudden he would give me a lovely present, though I would have preferred to have the money.

'When I got pregnant, he was furious. He'd thought I was on the Pill. But he hadn't asked, so I hadn't told him. Anyhow, he calmed down and became quite kind. When George was born, he seemed really proud, but he never asked me to marry him.

'While I was pregnant, he started giving me £5 a week and he's kept it up ever since. But I don't think it's for George. I think it's because he feels it gives him a right to the use of my . . . I was going to say cunt, but that's the point.'

'Just go on giving me the story straight, otherwise we might become a bit mixed up if you go off the track a little,' I suggested.

'All right,' she said. 'He qualified just after George was born, and got a job as a dental surgeon in a hospital in the West Country. But he came up to London every Friday evening, and stayed until Sunday night.

'He changed, too. He had been quite kind in his own way until George was born, but now he became cruel. By the way, he made me go on the Pill. I don't know what had happened to him, but to begin with he had difficulty in getting stiff. Then one night he demanded to fuck me in the anus.

'I don't like that, Dr Chartham. I tried to put him off, but he said that since George came, I had become too big and he couldn't feel anything. Anyhow, at last I said all right, I'd let him do it just once.

'As soon as I said yes, his cock got as stiff as a ram-rod. I made him use some baby cream, because I thought it might hurt if he tried to get in dry. He never lubricated very much.

Philip lubricated so much that when we first went together I thought he was coming off. Anyhow, I don't think I need have bothered, because the only sensation I got was a kind of tickling and, of course, I didn't come, which was no good to me, and after he'd come he still wouldn't help me.

'After that he wouldn't have me any other way. I'm being really honest when I say I don't like the idea of it, and I certainly don't like the act itself. But if I don't let him do it, he beats me up, and that seems to make him randier. Although he's so slim, he is quite strong, and he gets a terrible glassy look in his eyes when he is beating me, and he gets really aroused.

'I'm afraid of him now, because each time he beats me harder and he's threatened to take George away from me. It's funny, though – his bank still sends me £5 a week.

'I've moved twice, but each time he has found me. I wouldn't mind not getting his £5 a week if only I could be rid of him. Can you help me, please, Dr Chartham?'

'Just answer me one question, Mary,' I said. 'You say you've moved twice, so how has he found you?'

'I don't know,' she replied. 'That's the mystery.'

'Haven't you asked him?'

'I did once, and he just laughed.'

'You say you still get the £5 a week from his bank. How does that happen?'

'The landlady at my old room sends it on.'

'You've given her your new address?'

'Of course. That's how she knows where to send my letters.'

'And,' I said, 'you've told your dentist where he can find you.'

She was silent for a moment.

'Of course,' she said at last. 'You must think I'm very stupid, Dr Chartham.'

'Not stupid,' I said. 'Just a little unwise.'

'Can you help me?' she asked.

'Nothing more simple,' I said. 'I can promise you that you will never see him again, but you may not get the £5 a week if he remembers to cancel his banker's order, though

I'll try to frighten him into not doing so.'

All I had to do was to have my solicitor write to the dentist that, if he attempted to see Mary again, he would be reported to the General Dental Council.

Mary seemed greatly relieved.

'I have saved up £7, Dr Chartham,' she said, reaching for her handbag.

'Buy something nice for yourself and George with it,' I said, standing up to show her out of the room.

At the door she paused, then turned to me and said, 'But then there's the stealing.'

'The stealing!' I exclaimed.

'Yes,' she said.

'Perhaps you'd better come back and tell me all about it,' I suggested.

So she did.

To be fairly brief, she had fallen in love with Philip and had come to rely on their Saturday night encounters. When he had suddenly disappeared she had begun to steal from shops – in other words, she had become a shoplifter.

She had stopped when she had met George's father and had not shoplifted again until after George was born. But when the dentist had begun to insist on anal intercourse, she had started again.

'It's just as well you didn't go out of the room,' she said, 'because if you had I would probably have slipped your ashtray into my bag.'

'If you like it, have it,' I told her.

'I don't smoke,' she said, and went on, 'On the way here I went into Jackson's.' Jackson's were the grocers to the Queen. 'I can't afford to shop at Jackson's, and I shouldn't have gone in there,' she said.

'And what did you lift?' I asked, giving a small grin which was partly nerves, because I had never been consulted by a shoplifter before, and because I found the calmness of her confession endearing.

'A box of steel wool for scouring pans and a packet of *bouquet garnis*.'

'Which obviously you need at home,' I suggested.

She almost shouted. 'No! I don't need the bloody things.'

'Have you ever been caught?' I asked.

'I have six convictions, and I've been to prison for three months. Fortunately, a kind friend looked after George, but now I'm scared, because if I'm caught again, they will send me to prison for a year, at least, and George will be taken away from me and put into care. That I couldn't bear.'

'Then doesn't this thought stop you from stealing?' I asked.

'No, it doesn't. I wish to God it did! Dr Chartham, what am I going to do?'

We talked about her problem a little longer and the obvious pattern began to emerge – she shoplifted as a compensation for not being loved. So long as she did not have a man's affection – however spurious the affection might be – she had a compulsion to shoplift. When the dentist had demanded only anal intercourse with her, she had decided he no longer had any affection for her and, of course, she had been right, since he began to beat her when she tried to resist. What she was doing was to throw out distress signals that she needed not just attention, but love as well. Even counterfeit love would do.

This was something outside my capability to solve, because it needed special expertise and also a very long-term and very close counselling relationship.

In Britain, there is an organisation known as the Samaritans, founded mainly as a life-line for would-be suicides. Any potential suicide can ring a telephone number and talk to a trained counsellor, who will try to dissuade the victim of depression from carrying out self-murder. From a small beginning in the crypt of a London church, the Samaritans have spread all over the country, and their services have become much more diffused, until now they will undertake to counsel any kind of psychological problem.

Over the years the Samaritans and I had collaborated a good deal; they take my cases which needed intimate, long-term counselling, and I accept their more difficult cases of sexual dysfunction which have psychological

causes. (The Samaritans, by the way, give their services free.)

At once I telephoned the Samaritans, explained Mary's case to the assistant director, who was also a friend of mine, and made an initial appointment for her. The Mary who left my consulting-room was radiant; quite different from the Mary who had come in.

The London Samaritans were wonderful. She formed a psychological relationship with her counsellor and her urge to shoplift became less frequent. But then, for some reason or other which I have never been able to extract from her, she moved with baby George to the north-west. But she still kept in touch with me.

For about nine months she lived with a man whom she adored. During this period she did not steal one single thing. But when he was killed in a motor-car accident, she went to pieces again, and I received a frantic message from her saying that she was 'in trouble again'.

I urged her to get in touch with the local branch of the Samaritans, and arranged for her to see them. They worked wonders, too, until she quarrelled with her counsellor over a stupid and unimportant issue.

Then I got another message: 'I'm on my eleventh shoplifting charge. This time they *will* take George away from me.'

My lawyer arranged for a local advocate to defend Mary, at my expense. By the greatest of good luck, the police records of her previous convictions had not caught up with her, and she was given a suspended sentence.

This was a few months ago.

George is now ten, and a fine boy. Every month I receive a progress report on him – and herself – from Mary.

Sometime or other, I feel that her luck is going to run out, unless she forms a relationship with a man who has only to 'appear' to love her. That is the only permanent solution to her problem. At the moment this has not happened.

So long as her letters arrive, I am happy.

5 'Only with My Feet in Cold Water'

ONE DAY in the summer of 1950, a small party of boys were enjoying a swim in a pool which was secluded enough for them to swim in the nude. Among them was Jack, who was 12. He did not give the impression that he was shy and, in fact, he was not, until some of the older boys got into sexual horseplay, and were soon involved in mutual masturbation. These older boys, whose penises were crowned with hair, started ejaculation competitions to see who could come first or whose semen would shoot the furthest.

Jack did not join in these games, chiefly because he did not know exactly what his companions were doing. Certainly he was relieved to see that, within a few minutes of starting to play with each other's penises or their own, those members had become hard and upstanding.

Recently he had become aware that his own penis sometimes became stiff and stood up, and there would be strange feelings high up between his legs and his balls and the lower part of his belly, but he did not know that you could make it so stiff by rubbing it with your fingers, or why you should want it to be stiff. He had never played with his – it became hard and pointed up to the bedroom or bathroom ceiling by itself – and it had never occurred to him to rub it when it was hard.

He stood watching the scene fascinated. Presently he moved closer to a couple of the older boys who were competing with one another to see who could come first.

Although the sun was shining warmly, the water in which he stood was so cold that he could only just feel his feet and halfway up his calves.

Presently one of the boys cried out, and at that moment Jack was amazed to see a stream of milky-white droplets

'How do you do it?' he asked.

'Like me to show you?' Peter suggested.

'Yes, please,' said Jack.

So Peter stood half behind him, his left arm over Jack's left shoulder and his body pressing against Jack's.

More than ten years later Jack was to remember Peter's smooth skin moving against his and the movement of Peter's erection against the top of his right buttock. But most he was to remember the sensation of Peter's fingers gently enclosing his swollen penis and the movement of his foreskin, as Peter moved it backwards and forwards over his penis-head.

'You'll have these great feelings,' Peter said. 'At least, I hope you will. There'll be something wrong with you if you don't. And your cock will throb a few times. You must tell me when the throbbing stops, because if I go on rubbing after that, it will make your cock hurt. All right?'

'All right!' Jack agreed.

It had never occurred to him that anything could be so pleasant as jerking off. No wonder boys liked doing it.

After a minute or two, Peter asked, 'Getting any feelings yet?'

'I don't think so. It's nice, though. What are the feelings like?'

'Can't say exactly. They're like a big feeling of warmth which seems to start in your balls and then, like I said, spreads up to your belly and down through your thighs. They begin slowly, and then burst over you – it's like a flower opening quickly, I suppose,' Peter said poetically.

'I don't feel anything like that yet, but it's nice,' Jack repeated.

Then a minute or two later, he felt the first *frisson* as a strange warmth enveloped his testicles, and grew warmer, as Peter rubbed; it crept up into his belly and spread down into his thighs. Then the throbbing began, and each throb became stronger than the last, and his heart beat faster, and he felt he was going to burst.

At last there was a great throb and with it the warmth

seemed to rush down to his toes, and his toes and calves were tingling with the heat and the very cold water in which he was standing.

He tried to say 'Stop!' but he was panting so much he could not get the word to pass his lips. But his penis was beginning to hurt as Peter continued to rub it, so he jerked back with his buttocks, almost freeing his penis from Peter's hand. Peter understood, and took his hand away, asking, 'Have you come off?'

'I think so,' Jack replied. 'I had terrific feelings. They went right down to my toes.'

'I thought you were spending,' Peter said, 'by the noise you were making and the faces you were pulling.'

'Does everyone make noises and pull faces when they – er – spend?' Jack asked.

'Not everybody does. Phil over there – you can't tell what's happening to him until he shoots. But he does shoot quite a long way. I don't make much noise, though I do make some. I don't shoot so far as Phil, but I make more spunk. Were you kidding when you say you haven't jerked yourself off?'

'No, I'm not. But I'm sorry I haven't, because it was fantastic!'

'Now you know, you can have a lot of fun with yourself. You're a nice kid. Would you like to rub me up? It's nicer when somebody else does it for you.'

'I'd like to,' Jack said, feeling that at last he was grown up.

There were a lot of questions he would have liked to have asked Peter, but he was shy. Perhaps if he rubbed Peter up well, they could be friends, despite the wisps of hair surmounting Peter's cock, and Peter would tell him.

'Let's go and lie down over there,' Peter suggested. 'My feet are getting bloody cold, and it's nicer when you're lying down, I think.'

So they went up out of the water, and Peter chose a comfortable place in the long grass, and they lay down.

'Tell me if I'm not doing it right,' Jack said.

'I will,' Peter told him.

'OK,' Jack agreed.

They dressed and played with the trains for a time. Then they got bored, and after a little while longer, Jack said, 'I wouldn't mind a swim.'

'A good idea,' Peter agreed. So they got on their bicycles and rode to the pool. There was no one else there.

'I suppose everyone else is playing cricket or something,' Peter said as he undressed.

The water was no warmer than it had been before. Jack caught his breath as he plunged in, and Peter let out a yell, but after swimming about for a few minutes they were tingling from head to foot.

Presently Jack stood up and began to wade to shore. Almost as soon as he did so, Peter stood up, too, and called out, 'How can you get a hard-on when it's so cold?'

Jack looked down and saw that he really did have an erection.

'Didn't know I had one!' he called back.

Peter came splashing towards him. 'I've got an idea,' he said. 'Is your cock still sore?'

'No,' Jack told him, tentatively.

'Let me rub you up, then, and let's see what happens.'

'What, here?' Jack asked.

'Yes.'

'OK,' Jack replied.

So Peter stood behind him, as he had the first time, and began to stimulate Jack's penis. And presently the sensations began and as Peter rubbed, they increased and after a few minutes they came surging through his belly, his loins, his balls and his cock, so intensely that this time he had to cry out.

'There you are,' Peter said triumphantly, and they lay down in the sun to dry off. 'You can do it!'

'But why here and not on my bed or on yours?' Jack asked.

'I don't know,' Peter confessed. 'I'll ask my brother.'

That night when he went to bed, Jack tried to bring himself off again, but had to stop when his arm ached and his penis became sore. On Sundays his parents stayed in

bed longer than they did on weekdays. Jack woke with an erection and he began to pleasure himself, but with no more success than before. After a time, he got out of bed and went to the bathroom. He drew six inches or so of cold water into the bath, then he took off his pyjamas, got into the bath and sat on the edge with his feet in the water, and began to masturbate.

A few minutes passed, then to his great delight he knew he was going to come off, and presently he did. After that, whenever he wanted to masturbate, he would draw cold water into the bath and either stand in it or sit on the edge of the bath until he reached orgasm.

Fifteen years later Jack came into my consulting-room one afternoon. He was tall, broad-shouldered and very good-looking. Very attractive to women, was my first reaction.

He sat down and we chatted for a minute or two about things in general, and then I said, 'Well, what's this "funny problem" you referred to in your letter?'

'It *is* funny,' he said. 'You see, I can only come off when I have my feet in cold water.'

His answer took me by surprise, and to my lasting disgrace, I laughed. When I had checked myself and apologised ('I don't blame you, doctor. It is bloody ridiculous, isn't it?'), I said – the only thing I could think of immediately – 'That must limit positions.'

'Too right!' he said. 'I sit on the edge of the bath with my feet in cold water and my partner sits on me. I suppose I could have a basin of cold water in the bedroom. I tried it once or twice, but I spilled a lot of water. My wife got so fed up she divorced me, and my present girl-friend, although she's sympathetic, is beginning to show the same signs and I badly want to marry her.'

It was at once obvious that something had happened in childhood or adolescence which had brought about this strange complex, but I was nevertheless surprised when he told me the story I have just related.

Psychiatrists, especially Freudian or neo-Freudian ones, maintain that, if a person suffers the effects of a complex, as

soon as the causes of the complex are known by the patient, the complex disappears. I have never accepted this, because for the last half-century and more, I have been the victim of a psychological complex, the origins of which – the incident that triggered it off – I can pin-point to the hour, the actual day and the specific act. Its effects, however, have been with me all these years. (It has nothing at all to do with sex.)

Jack's story confirmed me in my disbelief of this theory, and I realised that I could do very little for him. He needed expert psychiatric treatment to undo the childhood 'imprinting' which was making his adult sexlife so difficult.

I explained this to him and told him that I would make arrangements for him to attend our most famous psychiatric institute. I had professional friends there who, I knew, would be interested in his case, which in my experience was unique. He was very grateful and shook me warmly by the hand.

He was just about to open the door to let himself out, when I had a brain-wave.

'Jack,' I called to him. 'Come back and sit down for a minute.'

Looking puzzled he did so.

'I've had an idea. Did you notice my receptionist when you came in?'

'Could anyone not?'

'Did she attract you?'

'You must be joking,' he smiled. 'The old loins began to rumble just glancing at her.'

'Would you like to have it off with her?' I asked.

'Are you serious?'

'Of course.'

'When?'

'Now. She acts as a surrogate for me. She's almost the most skilful woman at making love I know.'

He shook his head. 'I can think of nothing I'd like more,' he said, 'but it wouldn't be any good unless you have a bathroom handy.'

'We'll see,' I said. 'I'd like to try this experiment. It may

work, it may not. If it doesn't, no harm will have been done.'

'OK,' he grinned. 'This is an unexpected bonus.'

So I buzzed the intercom and asked Sylvia to come in. I introduced them and gave Sylvia a brief outline of Jack's story and his situation. There was no need to ask if she would be prepared to give Jack a helping hand.

'What precisely do you want me to do?' she asked.

'Get all the ice out of the refrigerator and put it in a plastic bag and seal it up so well so that the water doesn't drip out if the ice melts. Then put the bag in that ice container which we use for drink parties, and put it on the table within easy reach.

'Then I want you to make love to Jack in your incomparable fashion. Sometimes he feels he might come, but never does. Pull out all the stops and try to get him to this point.'

Turning to Jack, I said, 'If you ever do get to this point, I want you to tell Sylvia, and I want you to go into her. I want you to thrust away for some minutes, just to see if you can come off. I don't think you'll ever have been made love to before like Sylvia will make love to you. If you feel you are not going to come, tell Sylvia and stop thrusting. When he does that, Sylvia, get the ice-bag out of the box and, as quickly as possible, put it down at the bottom of the bed where he can put his feet on it. Understand what I mean, both of you?'

They said they understood.

'Jack,' I went on, 'if it's at all possible, I'd like you to get the bag in position without coming out of Sylvia. But if you find you cannot, it doesn't matter. Just get back into her as quickly as possible and continue thrusting with your feet on the bag. OK?'

'I see what you're getting at now, doctor,' Jack said.

'Right,' I smiled. 'Sylvia, you get the ice and I'll take Jack to the bedroom.'

'Get undressed while you're waiting and lie on the bed,' I told him. 'Sylvia wears so little, she just steps out of it in a

couple of seconds. Let me know what happens. I hope it works!'

I left the bedroom and went to the bathroom, and swung the first-aid cupboard, which concealed the back of the two-way mirror, away from it, so that I could watch what was happening on the bed. I also switched on the sound.

Within a couple of minutes, Jack was naked and lying on the bed, already with a fully fledged erection. He began to fondle himself as he looked round the room, but stopped abruptly and smiled guiltily as Sylvia came suddenly into the room with the ice-box.

I heard her say merrily – I don't think she has any inhibitions – 'You needn't stop for me, Jack. I like to watch a man wanking. It turns me on.'

'It doesn't do any good,' Jack said, 'but it's comforting.'

I felt really sorry for him and hoped that, if my idea didn't work, someone would be able to do something for him.

I always marvelled at the speed with which Sylvia undressed. One moment she was neatly dressed in her white overall and cap, and the next she was naked, her clothes about her feet. Of course, she did not wear stockings or tights and did not have to struggle with a girdle, and with one quick movement of a hand behind her back, her strapless bra literally flew off. I swear she was naked, on the bed beside Jack and caressing him within two minutes of entering the room.

It seemed to me that she must have been very attracted to Jack, or was in a really randy mood, because I could tell that she was already turned on when she lay down beside him and put his hand between her spread legs. He was a lucky young man, because Sylvia rarely displayed a passion to be on the receiving-end.

As I had asked her to do, she really did 'pull out all the stops', and she got Jack to the point of asking her if he could go in her.

'Oh, yes, please!' she said intensely.

She helped him in and he began thrusting. From his vocalising (which I could see was quite unconscious), I could tell that his orgasmic sensations were becoming quite

strong, and for some minutes I thought he might come off naturally. Sylvia must have thought so, too, because she did all she could with words and actions to encourage him.

But it was no good.

Presently, he collapsed, gasping, on to Sylvia. 'I'm sorry,' he said, between pants. 'I thought I was going to make it.'

'Lie still!' commanded Sylvia. 'Go on thrusting gently!' and she reached out to the ice-box and extracted the bag.

They had a little difficulty in getting the bag to where Jack's feet could rest on it, and I had to join in their hilarity. (I doubt whether Jack had ever laughed while making love before. It was good, because it relaxed him.) However, at least they got it into place, though not without Jack having to withdraw, which surprised me, because his penis, I judged, was over-average in length.

As soon as Jack had fully penetrated her again, Sylvia reached down between their bodies and cupped his balls in her hand. I am sure Jack had never experienced this exquisite caress before, because he purred like a satisfied bear.

Then he began to thrust, and it was clear that he had reactivated his orgasmic sensations from the sounds he uttered and by the faster movements of his buttocks.

All of a sudden, he thrust fully into Sylvia and stayed there, with his buttocks taut and his torso lifted away from Sylvia's, supported on his rigid arms. From the expression on the side of his face which I could see, I could tell that his teeth were clenched and his lips drawn back from them.

He remained in this posture for more than a minute, during which Sylvia was making her customary exciting orgasmic sounds. Then he went limp and collapsed on her.

A few seconds later he gasped, 'Oh my God! That was good!' There was a pause, then he almost shouted, 'I've come off for the first time in bed,' and rolled off Sylvia, his penis, though limp, still heavily swollen.

He was quiet for a time, lying beside her, his arm across his eyes.

'God!' he said presently. 'You're a good . . .' My heart

came into my mouth, because Sylvia does not like being told that she is 'a good lay'.

He stopped abruptly. 'Darling,' he said, 'you're such a good lover. Won't you marry me?'

Sylvia replied in her loving-but-matter-of-fact voice, 'Sorry, darling, I'm already committed. But if your girl-friend would like a few tips, send her to me.'

A little later they came back into my consulting-room.

'Well?' I asked.

'It worked . . . worked . . . worked!' Jack exclaimed, oblivious of the fact that I had seen and listened to it all.

'Marvellous!' I replied enthusiastically. 'I'd like you to go home and repeat it with your girl-friend. Do you have ice at home?'

'Of course!' he said.

'Let me know what happens, either way, please,' I said.

I felt fairly certain that we had broken through his psychological barrier to making love naturally. But one can never be sure after just one incident.

You can imagine my delight when a week later he wrote to me saying, 'We've fucked ourselves silly. I don't even need the ice-bag now.'

A month later, Sylvia and I received a wedding invitation which was the greatest compliment of all.

6 Falling Out of Love with Sex

FRANK AND Mary are 25 and 23 respectively. Frank had had a little sexual experience, and Mary none, when they got engaged. They had to wait for a year for the house they were buying to be finished. They decided not to get married before they moved in, but they could see no reason why their deferred wedding should prohibit them from making love in the meantime.

At the beginning, Mary was a little afraid that they were going to be sexually incompatible. 'I didn't think I was going to be able to keep up with Frank, but as time went by, I found I was liking sex more and more, and Frank was always delighted whenever I made the first move.'

Mary decided she would go on working until they wanted to have a baby, because her money would help while they were getting established. They thought they would start a family when they had been married two or three years.

They had been married eight or nine months when Mary came to see me. Three months or so after the wedding, Frank had admitted that he was going off sex. He couldn't explain why: he just didn't feel like it nowadays like he used to.

Mary was upset, because she thought he was falling out of love with her. While they were engaged, he often gave her little presents – chocolates, a bracelet, ear-rings, flowers – now he never bought her anything.

When she tackled him about it, 'he got quite shirty, and told me not to be stupid. Of course he still loved me. Why was I always harking on about sex? He'd come to the conclusion it was very much over-rated.'

They were not flush with money; they had to be careful, but they were not worried about it. Certainly, running a house was proving to be a little more expensive than they had thought it would, and they would probably have to put

off starting a family for a year or two longer than they had intended. But Frank was studying for exams which would give him promotion.

'He doesn't have to work very hard at studying, because he's really quite clever. I had thought of that, too, Dr Chartham, but I don't see that it can be the reason. He taught me to need sex, and now he doesn't help me. What are we going to do?'

Sandra, 21, had been married about six months when she came to me. She and Richard had lived together for seven months before they married.

'Our lovemaking was wonderful then. Neither of us is inhibited in any way, and I imagine we've tried almost everything. So it can't be boredom. I just don't feel I want sex any more. I let Richard make love to me, but I have to force myself. He realises I've changed, and he doesn't get so much satisfaction as he used to, and he's becoming frustrated. It's really getting on both our nerves, which is why I've come to you. I can see us breaking up if I don't do something. What's wrong with me?'

Jane is 27. She had a good job and was heading for a junior executive position when she married Mark, who insisted she must give up her job because it would be bad for his image at the office if it was thought he couldn't support his wife.

They had made love while they were engaged, and both had enjoyed it. 'We agreed to go by what you say, Dr Chartham, and use sex to express our love for one another. From what one hears, I don't suppose we were very adventurous, but Jane agreed with me that it couldn't really be better. I'm certainly not bored with it, and Jane assures me she isn't bored either.

'It's just that she doesn't want to make love now as often as we used to. It's a struggle to get her to co-operate once a week. At the beginning, we never made love less than four times a week. So surely she must be bored. And yet she won't try out the new positions and so on that I've sug-

gested. It's making me kinky, Dr Chartham. Do you know that I've gone back to masturbating?'

'Yes,' I told him. 'Most married men do, even when they are happily having sex with their wives. What does Jane do with herself all day?'

'She looks after the house. She's a good wife in every other respect, but she spends an awful lot of time with her mother, and I'm wondering if that might have something to do with it.'

These are some cases that I have selected from 22 similar ones which have come my way in the last 18 months, and most of them are frankly puzzling. I wish they were all as easy to solve as Jane's, where we discovered, after some probing, that she was resentful of Mark because he had made her give up her job, and she was unconsciously punishing him by withholding herself sexually from him. In far too many other cases, I have been completely unsuccessful.

In my experience, this 'falling out of love with sex' is a fairly recent phenomenon. The eminent sociologist, Michael Schofield has noted in his survey, *The Sexual Behaviour of Young Adults*, that 17 per cent of those in his sample who were married admitted to losing interest in or becoming bored with sex. Unfortunately, from my point of view, he does not say whether these people had made love regularly before marriage, or how long after marriage they had begun to lose interest or were bored.

I have given a good deal of thought to this, and have not yet come up with a satisfactory answer. But among my speculations are:

(1) the Pill, some brands of which are known to lessen sexual desire in some women after they have been on it for some months.
(2) that sex before marriage is satisfactory and satisfying, because it is a new experience and, therefore, exciting, but that after marriage its ready availability takes some of the gilt off the gingerbread.

(3) that married life turns out to be very different even from living together before marriage, and that the responsibilities of running and supporting a home have a dampening effect on sexual desire.
(4) that hitherto unnoted hormonal changes are affecting the sexual desire of young men, though it is difficult to assess why the changes take place at this early period of maturity.
(5) that before marriage both partners are trying to impress upon each other their desirability as sexual partners in order to acquire the other as a marriage partner, and when the partner has been acquired in marriage, there is no longer any incentive to impress, with a consequent falling off in performance and then in desire.
(6) that the general stresses and strains of these modern times, which increase as one grows older, are now beginning to take effect, by sapping sexual energy, at an earlier age than hitherto.
(7) that there are far more special cases, like Jane's, than we have ever discovered before.

It is an interesting and important question, and I should be happy to hear from anyone who has experienced any lessening in sexual desire and interest after having been married for one or two years, or after having lived with a partner on a regular basis for a similar period.

7 A Case of Fear

ONE MORNING about 15 years ago, when Margaret was five, her parents were making love. They were highly aroused and so engrossed in their activity that they did not hear their bedroom door open, and Margaret come in. A second or two later, her father mounted her mother and began to thrust. Her mother was crying out in ecstasy, and her father was replying, though Margaret could not recall what he was saying. (I doubt whether she ever knew.)

'I was quite sure that Daddy was attacking Mummy,' Margaret told me at our first session, 'so I ran to the bed and shouted to him to stop.'

'And did he stop?'

'Yes. Both of them looked at me, startled, and Daddy rolled off Mummy, and as he did so I saw this long, stiff, thick stick come out of her. Then I realised it wasn't a stick which he was beating her with, but his penis, which I had often seen before, only then it had been hanging down, and once, when he had let me touch it, it had been very soft. Now it was twice as long and twice as thick, and was hard and stood up straight and away from his body.

'I was so horror-struck by the size of it that I could not take my eyes off it, and although I knew that they were both angry and talking to me, I could not move. Even when Mummy got off the bed and picked me up and carried me out of the room, scolding me, I remember looking over her shoulder at Daddy's erection.'

'Did they ever explain to you that they were not fighting, but were loving one another in a special way?' I asked.

'No, they didn't. But after that, when I went to their room sometimes, the door was locked, and I could hear

them making noises and the sound of the bed shaking.'

'How old were you when you realised what they were doing?'

She thought for a moment. 'Twelve, I imagine,' she said eventually. 'I began to menstruate when I was just turned 12, and Mummy told me all about sex. I was horrified when she told me that the man puts his erect penis right inside the woman's vagina.

'I asked her, "Are all men's penises as big as Daddy's when they are stiff?" She smiled and said, "I'd forgotten about that morning. Daddy's penis isn't all that big. There are bigger."

' "I'll never be able to get one half the size of Daddy's inside me," I told her. "Of course you will. Vaginas stretch, and will take any size of penis." '

'That's more or less correct,' I told Margaret. 'Most vaginas take any thickness of penis, but in some cases where the man has a penis longer than 20 to 25 centimetres – eight to ten inches – it can be painful for the woman to take the whole length. Penises of this length, however, are very, very rare and the man who has such a long one learns very early in his sexual life a technique of not fully penetrating a vagina.'

'What is the average size of a penis?' she asked.

'Fifteen to 16 centimetres long,' I told her, 'and just over 11 centimetres in circumference.'

'Then Allan's is about average,' she commented.

'Who is Allan?' I asked.

'My boy-friend,' she replied. 'I've fallen in love with him and I want to marry him, but I can't let him make love to me because I'm afraid his penis is going to hurt me. That's why I've come to see you.'

'Tell me more,' I said.

'About what?' she asked.

'About this fear of yours.'

'I've always had it since Mummy told me that the penis goes into the vagina, and I recalled how big Daddy's looked.'

'But you were a little girl then,' I reminded her. 'Every-

thing, not just penises, look bigger than they are to small children.'

'I know all that,' she replied, 'but it still doesn't make me able to let Allan come into me.'

'Is Allan your first boy-friend?'

'I've had several, but they all said goodbye when I refused to let them make love to me.'

'So you're still a virgin?'

'Naturally! But, believe me, Dr Chartham, I don't want to be, especially with Allan. I really love him, and he turns me on so much . . . Ever since I met him, I've been masturbating a lot more.'

'How often do you masturbate?' I asked.

'I used to masturbate every day, but now I bring myself off at least twice, and frequently more often.'

'Would you say you were fairly highly sexed?'

'I don't know. How do you tell?'

'How often do you feel randy? Every day?'

'A minimum.'

This was going to make things much more difficult for her in solving her problem.

'How do you know how big Allan's penis is?'

'We went to bed. I honestly wanted to go all the way with him, and I tried very hard – and succeeded – not to look at his penis. I thought if I didn't see how big it was, I might be able to manage. But, of course, he wanted me to play with it and, of course, you have to, when you're making love, don't you?'

I smiled. 'It's nicer for your partner if you do . . . So?'

'It felt enormous, and so stiff – like a steel rod! When he asked me if I was ready, I knew I couldn't let him come in me, and I began to cry. Naturally, he wanted to know why, and gradually he coaxed my fears out of me. When I said his penis felt huge, he said I must be joking.

' "Have you a tape-measure?" he asked.

'I got a measure from my work-basket, and then, of course, I had to look at his penis when he measured it.'

'What did it measure?' I asked her.

'Fifteen centimetres long and 12½ round. But it still

looked menacing,' she replied. 'We tried all sorts of things, but I just couldn't let him bring that big stick of his anywhere near my vagina. At last we gave up, but I think he must love me, too, because instead of going away like the others, he's kept on seeing me and it's because of him that I am here to see you.'

'It's a pity,' I said, 'that your parents didn't always lock the bedroom door when they were making love, if you were in the habit of dropping by to see them.' And I explained to her that it might have helped had her parents quietened her. 'But they did not, so we must see what we can do.'

Freud, as I have previously said, maintained that if you know the cause of a psychological 'block', the 'block' will disappear. Throughout my counselling experience, I have come across cases where the cause of the 'block' was known, and yet the 'block' remained. Now here was Margaret in the same category.

However, knowing the cause of the 'block' might help in Margaret's treatment which, I believed, would have to be a mixture of physical and psychological. We had to convince her that her vagina would accept *comfortably* – that was the key word – any penis of reasonable size, say up to 18.5 centimetres in length and 15 centimetres in circumference.

In case you don't know the details, the vagina is a tube which consists of three layers. The inner one – the lining, with which the penis comes into contact when it enters the vagina – is a mucous membrane, a special kind of skin which lines interior organs, such as the mouth. The middle layer consists of erectile tissue, which allows the vagina to lengthen and swell under sexual arousal; while the outer layer is muscle. During sexual arousal, this muscle can contract, and in some women these contractions can be strong enough to be felt by the penis, especially during orgasm. (Nevertheless, the vaginal contractions of quite a high proportion of women are not strong enough to be felt, not only by the penis, but by the woman herself.)

On the other hand, the entrance to the vagina is a ring of muscle, known as a sphincter. Compared with the outer layer of the vaginal barrel, the sphincter is quite a strong

muscle, and in a fair proportion of women who have not had a child, it automatically contracts during orgasm, gripping and releasing the penis. The strength of the contractions varies from woman to woman, but no matter how weak the contractions, they can be made stronger by certain exercises.

In the Orient, women are taught to control their vaginal sphincter, because it is very exciting for the man, after coupling, to have his penis rhythmically squeezed. In the West, however, except for the perineum – the bridge between the base of the vagina and the anus – the vaginal sphincter is the most neglected part of the woman's sexual anatomy.

After my first experience of the use of the sphincter during coupling in Java (now Indonesia), I returned determined to make Western women aware of the marvellous technique of male arousal they had at their command, primarily because one of the chief complaints of husbands and lovers of women who have had several children is what is known as the 'slack vagina'. That is, the men feel they are not in close contact with the vagina during coupling.

I developed a method of training which would make the vaginal sphincter able to contract and relax at will. It is even possible to contract the sphincter to such an extent that it is possible for the woman to hold the penis prisoner, if she so wishes.

For this training, I used a set of five graduated glass tubes. The length of all tubes was 17.5 centimetres, but the circumference ranged between 8.75 and 13.75 centimetres. Training began with the largest and graduated to the smallest. If, when the woman had learned to grip 8.75 (the smallest) so firmly that her partner felt 'captivated', and she wanted to improve on this performance, I did not dissuade her. As a result, I have a number of patients who are able to have such a grip that if you insert a slim pencil into the vagina it cannot be withdrawn. (By the way, this is within the performance of 99.1 per cent of *all* women, if they wish to be regarded as the ultimate in lovers.)

In Margaret's case, I thought I would reverse my 'train-

ing' – begin with the thinnest and graduate to the thickest. I was not concerned, at this point, with her vaginal sphincter, but merely with getting her used to feeling a tube inside her.

I showed her the tube – 17.5 centimetres long and 8.75 centimetres thick, and assured her that I would not insert more than 8 centimetres.

The first session went off very well.

At the second session, I let her see the tube that was going to penetrate her, and this gave rise to her first problem – she would not believe that I would not insert more than 8 centimetres, and she was also convinced that the thickness would give her pain. So I said we would use the smallest tube, but this time I wanted to mask her. I'm afraid I cheated – I inserted the second tube, and she felt no difference and accepted it without complaint.

At subsequent sessions, I used this technique until, eventually, I was able to penetrate her with a special tube 18.75 centimetres long and 13.75 in circumference, with the end of the shaft being pressed right up against her vaginal lips.

At the end of this session, I unmasked her and said, 'I want you to draw the tube out yourself.'

She had a little difficulty in finding the rim of the tube with her fingertips, but eventually she did, and when she looked at it, she could not believe her eyes.

'You see,' I said, 'if you can take a tube this size without it hurting you, you can take a penis that is not quite so big.'

She agreed.

I asked her to let her boy-friend make love to her, but she was not ready for that.

'Have you seen George?' I asked her.

'Who's George?'

'One of my assistants,' I said. 'He might have been with Sylvia when you arrived.'

'Oh, yes. That quite good-looking boy. Why do you ask?'

'I'd like you to see one of George's tricks.'

'What does he do?'

'Like Maupassant, he can give himself an erection, just

by thinking about it, in less than half a minute,' I explained.

'So what will it do for me?' she asked.

'I'd just like you to see – *see* – the erection of another boy.'

'OK,' she said.

Over the intercom, I asked Sylvia if George were still there. She said he was on the point of leaving, but he could stay if I wanted him.

'Ask him to come in,' I told her.

A moment or two later there was a knock on the door and George came in.

'I'd like you to show Margaret your trick.'

'Of course.'

It took him less than a minute to strip off and stand before us naked, waiting for instructions. He had just had a training session with a patient, and his penis was hardly visible in its thick nest of hair.

'I'd like you to go and feel his penis,' I said to Margaret. 'I want you to be sure that it is completely soft and not threatening.'

'Threatening?' she asked.

'Yes – threatening!' I repeated.

She hesitated for a few seconds, then she went to George and began to fondle him.

'You see,' I said, 'how soft and companionable it is.'

She agreed.

'Right! Come back here by me . . . George, off you go! Watch carefully, Margaret.'

In less than half a minute, George was fully erect. From the soft, unthreatening tube of spongy tissue, able to be kneaded, his penis rose up stiff and strong and nodding – with pleasure?

'Go and take it in your hand,' I told Margaret. 'Just like you did when it was soft.'

She hesitated, but then went over to George and ran her hand up and down his penis.

'What do you think?' I asked.

'It depends on what you want me to say.'

'Do you accept it or reject it?'

'I'm afraid of it.'

'You find it threatening?'

'Yes, I think I do.'

I dismissed George, and when he had gone, I asked what she thought of the size of his erect penis.

'A bit big?' she queried.

'But nothing like so big as the tube you took out of your vagina just now.'

'Maybe,' she agreed. 'But it feels *immense*.'

We talked for a while, and at last agreed that the penis of her boy-friend Allan was not so big as George's penis, and that George's was not so big as the tube I had inserted in her that afternoon without the slightest pain.

Then I said, 'You told me that you can't make love all the way with Allan. Why not?'

She did not answer at once, then said, 'I don't really know . . . Yes, I do . . . I have this idea . . . I just cannot accept a huge rod of a penis . . . *it will hurt me!*'

'But the tube was much larger than any penis you have seen or touched.'

She nodded then, with a kind of desperation, cried, 'Oh, I don't know! Why have I come to see you?'

'Never mind for today. Come and see me again next week, and try not to worry.'

In the meantime I gave a good deal of thought to her case. We knew what the problem was, and we knew the cause of it. Somehow, I had to persuade her to accept a penis without any psychological difficulty.

I had a small collection of films of couples copulating which I used during counselling sessions sometimes to demonstrate a technique. For example, although you may not believe it, quite intelligent men and women often cannot understand the simple technique of getting the penis into the vagina just by a description in words.

So, when Margaret next appeared, I had selected two of these films. In both of them, the male had a penis that seemed to be, although I do not suppose it actually was – the camera *can* lie – larger than usual. My hope was that by showing her how these really large penises could glide into

the vagina, she might be encouraged at least to accept George's. But when I got her on the bed with George, she had an attack of vaginismus – her vagina closed tightly and George could not part her vaginal lips.

George was very upset, because it was the first time he had been 'rejected'. I was upset, too, because I thought it might give him a problem as well, but fortunately he had worked with me long enough to know about most problems, and in the event was not affected.

The following week, I arranged for Margaret to watch George and Sylvia making love, through the two-way mirror. She did not find it objectionable, so I suggested we went into the bedroom and watched them 'in the flesh' so to speak. I asked George to withdraw, and instructed Margaret to run her hand up and down his erect penis a few times. She did so without any bad reaction, but when George placed himself above Sylvia again, and Sylvia put his penis into her and he began to thrust, Margaret became quite violent. So violent, in fact, that we had to end the session.

Now I was at my wits' end.

Would her boy-friend take part in our experiments? She agreed to ask him to come and see me.

Allan was an attractive boy, and it was not difficult to discover that he was truly in love with Margaret. The three of us discussed her problem in a very adult way, but I could not help deciding at the end, that she had an age of 12 or 13 when it came to coupling.

Nevertheless, Allan came with her again on her next 'working' session. I put them to bed and watched them through the mirror.

Allan responded well, despite knowing that I was watching, and I had great hopes that he would succeed. But my hopes were to be dashed. As soon as he placed himself above her, even though she put down her hands to help him in, as soon as his penis-head came near her vaginal lips, she froze. We had to abandon the session, and a rather upset Allan went away.

I took Margaret back to the consulting-room, intending

to tell her that I could not help her any more, and that she must find another therapist who might be able to.

I had been looking for another male surrogate to replace a boy who had got married recently and whose wife had asked him not to go on working for me. My surrogates did occasionally leave me, but I rarely had any difficulty replacing them. I didn't even have to advertise; the word seemed to get around on the grapevine, and Sylvia would receive a telephone call. She knew the questions to ask, and she and George sorted out the more likely candidates, for me to interview.

As I was about to tell Margaret of my decision, the intercom buzzed, and Sylvia said, 'Peter, the new boy, is here.'

'Right!' I said. 'Show him into the bedroom, tell him to strip off and work up an erection, and I'll be with him in a minute or two.' (This is a good preliminary test, because some men have difficulty getting an erection 'to order', which is generally what surrogates have to do in their 'work' to be successful.)

Before I could return my attention to Margaret, she said, 'Do you think this new boy could help me?'

'I shouldn't think so,' I said. 'He's never done anything like this before and may take a little training.'

'But he knows how to make love?'

'Naturally, but I don't know how good he is.'

'May I have a look at him?'

In my job, I am never allowed to forget the perversity of women's behaviour, so I said, 'Yes, if you want to. But, honestly, I don't think it will do any good.'

We went into the bathroom and looked through the mirror. Peter had already stripped and was sitting on the edge of the bed facing us and coaxing his penis into erection. He *was* handsome and his penis was responding well. It was about the size of George's, which she had rejected, but suddenly I felt her hand gripping my arm like a vice.

'He's beautiful,' she whispered. 'I'd like to try with him.'

It occurred to me that by letting her have her wish

there was nothing to lose, and it would be a good test for him.

So I led her back to the consulting-room, told her to undress and go to the bedroom to see what happened. I noticed, as she took off her bra, that she was sexually aroused. Her nipples rose out of their areolae like miniature alpine peaks.

'All right,' I said, when she was completely naked. 'There's the door. He's all yours.'

As soon as the door to the bedroom closed behind her, I hurried into the bathroom and switched on the sound. Peter, who has become my most successful assistant after George – who is unbeatable – looked up startled, but I could see by the nodding of his now fully erect penis, as he stood up and faced her, that he had been fully turned on by the sight of her.

She ran to him, pushed him on to the bed, flung herself beside him, exclaiming hoarsely and urgently, 'Fuck me! Fuck me! Fuck me!'

Afterwards Peter told me that he had thought this challenge was part of the test which Sylvia had told him he would have to take. He took Margaret at her word, and without uttering a sound, flung himself upon her, guided his penis into her vagina skilfully and swiftly, and thrust and thrust to the accompaniment of her noisy struggles to be free of him.

When both had come off, and were lying breathlessly side by side, I went into the bathroom.

'I'm Robert Chartham,' I said, shaking Peter's hand. 'Welcome.'

'Have I passed?' he asked.

'We'll talk about that later. But yes! Have no fear! You've just performed a miracle.'

'What do you mean?' he asked, puzzled.

'I'll tell you all about it in a few minutes. Do you think you could get another hard-on?'

'I think so,' he said, and in a couple of minutes of stimulation, he had.

'Look, Margaret!' I told her. 'Feel it and play with it. It's

much larger than Allan's. If you can take Peter, you can take Allan.'

And so it turned out.

Less than a week later, Allan rang me up. 'What have you done to Margaret? I'm having difficulty satisfying her,' he told me.

'Are you complaining?' I laughed.

'Come to the wedding,' he laughed back. 'And many thanks.'

8 Not Like the Others

TIM WAS 17 when he wrote to me asking if he could see me, provided my fee was not more than £10. He was still at an English public school, and he had managed to save the sum he mentioned out of his pocket-money. He hoped I would accept that, because he desperately needed my advice. He had read one or two of my books, and was a regular reader of *Forum*, which was passed round among the seniors at school, and he felt that I was the only one with whom he would like to discuss his problem.

I wrote back, telling him that I would see him for free and giving him an appointment. 'If you cannot get away from school,' I told him, 'please telephone my receptionist, and we'll fix you up in the holidays, if you can wait that long. If we don't hear from you, we shall take it for granted that you can come at the appointed time.'

We didn't hear from him, and he arrived at the appointed time.

It was a sturdy, good-looking – although not actually handsome – boy whom Sylvia showed into the consulting-room. Not tall, but broad-shouldered and, as we say, glowing with rude health. Just what a teenager should be who lives a smokeless, non-alcoholic and drugless life.

By way of introduction, and to put him at his ease, I asked him how he had managed to get away from school on an afternoon in the middle of the week.

'As easy as falling off a log, sir,' he grinned. 'When you become a prefect you may go out whenever you like, provided you attend a few classes and get your work done properly. All you have to do is to sign the House Book before you go out and sign it again when you come in.'

'As easy as that!' I commented, remembering my own strict school upbringing. 'They must have great faith in you!'

'I think they have, sir,' Tim replied. 'Mind you, if you do go out a great deal, it is noticed and the house-master sends for you, and wants to know why and where you've been. But you really are on your honour, and when you're on your honour, you keep to the rules, don't you?'

'So you don't go out without signing the book?' I smiled.

'Of course not, sir!' He sounded quite indignant.

'But you could,' I suggested, feeling somehow that I was not being very bright.

'Of course you could,' he agreed, 'but you would be an idiot to try it.'

'Why?'

'Because you never know when someone may want you, the Head or a tutor, for something or other, and if you can't be found and your name isn't in the book, you will most certainly suffer for it.'

'Physically?' I asked, recalling my own beatings.

'You're talking about the Dark Ages, sir!' he smiled.

'Of my own schooldays!' I admitted.

'No, not physically, but by the loss of all kinds of privileges. Sir, are you sure you won't take a fee?'

He brought us back on track.

'Quite sure – teenagers and senior citizens, unless the latter are rich, not a bean!' I assured him. 'So what is your problem?'

A few weeks earlier he had had an attack of mumps which had made his testicles swell, as mumps very often does.

'Both?' I asked him.

'I don't know,' he said. 'My scrotum became the size of a medium-sized football.'

'Very frightening,' I said.

'I'll say . . . and very painful.'

'So?'

'Well, Dr Chartham, the school doctor says I'll never be able to have children. If that's true, what am I going to do?' There was real distress in his voice.

'Do you want children?' I asked. It was a silly question to ask a young male not yet out of school.

'I haven't really thought about it,' he admitted. 'But chaps do want children usually, don't they? Besides, if a chap can't have children, he's not really a man, is he?'

'I can't see why not,' I said. 'But that's a long story. Why are you really so keen on having children?'

'Family,' he said. 'I'm an only son. If I can't produce children, the family comes to an end. Dad wouldn't like that.'

'Has it ever struck you,' I asked, 'that if you can have children, you may have only girls?'

'No,' he said. 'I haven't got that far. I'm really rather scared. All I want to know is if the school doctor is right.'

'We can soon test that,' I told him.

'How?' he asked.

'Do you think you could wank off now?'

He looked puzzled.

'I believe so. But why?' he asked.

'If you can produce a specimen of semen for me, I'll have a look at it and tell you what I think,' I said.

'Honest?'

'Honest!'

'OK,' he said, 'I'll try! Are you going to stay?'

'No! Not unless you want me to.'

He thought for a moment.

'I don't really,' he said. 'But I could, because at school we have wanking parties.'

'I'm afraid I'm past that,' I smiled at him. I took a measuring glass from the cupboard. 'I'd like you to shoot into this,' I told him. 'Try not to miss a drop. I'm going to have a word with my receptionist. When you're ready, press this switch on the intercom and just say "OK".'

I left him to his own devices, and went to the reception to look at the appointments book, and to have a chat with Sylvia. I suppose five or six minutes went by, then the intercom on Sylvia's desk crackled, and Tim's voice said, 'OK.'

'OK,' I replied. 'I'll be there.'

When I went back into the consulting-room, he was impeccably and respectably dressed and on my desk was

the measuring glass containing 6.4 ml of semen, in other words, well above the mature male average of 5.0 ml. I was surprised by this, and asked him when he had ejaculated last.

'The day before yesterday,' he said.

'Would you mind if I inspected your testicles manually?' I asked him. 'This specimen is well above average in quantity. We've got to wait about 20 minutes for the semen to clear. Would you mind?'

'Certainly not,' he said. 'What shall I do?'

'Take off your jacket, trousers and underpants, and get up on the couch,' I told him. 'Do you want to go behind the screen?'

He laughed. 'Good heavens . . . why?'

'I thought you might be shy. A lot of people are until they've got their clothes off.'

He undressed without any sign of embarrassment whatsoever. The young generation of today have certainly got their attitudes to their privates right. What a psychologically healthy manifestation!

Remembering that he was only 17, I was surprised by the size of his scrotum and when I gently probed his testicles with my fingers, I was equally surprised. They were very large.

'Have they always been this size?' I asked him.

'Lately they have,' he said.

'Have the mumps left them like this?'

'Certainly not!' he said. 'I've always had heavy balls – like my father. What I meant by "lately" was that a few months ago they suddenly seemed to have got even bigger than they were. But that was long before the mumps.'

I am doubtful about the theory that there is a relationship between the size of the testicles and the amount of the ejaculate. I tend to think that the latter is controlled by the size of the seminal vesicles and their rate of fluid production, but it was very interesting to find a comparison in Tim's case.

I told him to get dressed again, and while we were waiting for the semen to clear, we chatted, and then he asked me if I

would see his friend Phillip, who had, as he put it, 'operational problems'. From what Tim told me, I decided to see his friend.

At length the semen was clear enough for me to inspect it under the microscope. The rough count which I was able to make after doing a few sums was 25 million very active sperm per cubic centimetre; quite enough for him to produce as many children as he wished, though in proportion to the quantity of semen, I believed that one of the testicles could have been affected by the mumps.

I asked him to look down the microscope at the spermatozoa threshing about in the fluid. He was not only amazed, but so relieved that he could hardly hold back his tears.

Inwardly I was angry with the school doctor, who was really not qualified to have given Tim this diagnosis, and certainly should not have been placed in a position of looking after and advising young males with these sorts of problems. The man had attempted no tests of Tim's semen, and had not even arranged for the boy to see a consultant, and although mumps affecting the testicles can, rarely, affect fertility in one way or another, unless both testicles are highly affected complete sterility cannot result. The doctor should *never*, but *never*, have told the boy that he would not be able to have children, whether or not the likelihood was, in fact, a certainty. When Tim proposed to marry was the time for tests to be carried out. Even then, marriage would depend on whether or not one or other of the couple wished to have children.

I did not explain any of this to Tim, but I did later write to his house-master.

We called in Sylvia and fixed an appointment for Tim's friend, Phillip, in a week's time.

As he said goodbye, Tim remarked, 'I knew you would be able to help me. But even if you had said I could never be a father, I would have been able to accept it, because I'm sure you would have explained it kindly, and I shouldn't have minded. You wouldn't have blurted it out like that idiot.'

Even after nearly half a century of counselling and

therapy, it is extremely gratifying to have so much trust placed in one – although, at the same time, very, very daunting – but coming from a virile boy on the threshold of manhood, it was even better to hear. We therapists, you know, are not always sure whether we are doing much good or not. It makes us happy to be told now and again that we have had a success.

Phillip, aged 18, *was* handsome. He was quite a bit taller than Tim, but not quite so broad in the shoulders. He would, I thought, be very acceptable to any well-discerning woman.

Tim must have set his mind at rest, because I could tell, as soon as Sylvia showed him in, that he was relaxed.

We talked a bit, and then I asked him what his problem was.

'It's difficult to explain,' he said.

'You come too soon?' I suggested.

'No, I don't come at all,' he said. Then he went on, 'It's very difficult to explain, Dr Chartham. All my friends are wanking away and having fun – but I can't.'

'What happens, then?' I asked, genuinely puzzled, because in such a situation one does not often find a young man to be impotent.

'Well,' he said, 'I can get it up and it's really stiff, but no matter what happens afterwards, within a couple of minutes, before I get anywhere near to coming, it goes "flop". Tim is a very good friend of mine. He read somewhere about an elastic band at the base of the shaft, and we tried that. But, no – flop it went. It's very embarrassing, because most of my friends know about it. Some who aren't my friends come to my room and wank off in front of me, just to tease me.'

'Has it always been like that?' I asked.

'So far as I can remember – yes. But . . .'

I clutched at the 'but'. 'But what?' I asked.

'I believe I dreamt it, but I have a kind of memory of wanking when I was quite young, and having very powerful sensations.'

I breathed a sigh of relief. If he had said he had had

absolutely no experience of what might have been orgasmic sensations, there was a possibility that he had been born orgasmically anaesthetic, and in my experience there is nothing that can be done about orgasmic anaesthesia.

From his family history, I discovered that Phillip's father had been a professional soldier, who had been killed on duty when Phillip had been so young that he could not remember him. Phillip had a sister a couple of years older, who had been expelled from her very expensive private girls' school for stealing. This, together with Phillip's story, made me think that there was the possibility of psychological instability within the family. The mother had not remarried. I met her later and found her to be a rational and psychologically well-balanced woman.

Phillip's 'kind of memory' of erection and orgasmic sensations could indicate that something extremely traumatic had happened to him, more than likely in prepubertal days. This could account for his present disastrous condition, and I began to question him along these lines.

After a couple of sessions I was certain that an adult had 'interfered' with him, but no matter how deeply I probed, we got nowhere. Even under medium-trance hypnosis, he did not respond at all.

I thought then, and I still think, that this case was as challenging as Jack's – the young man who could only reach orgasm if he had his feet in cold water. But I did not have such a quick success with Phillip as I had with Jack. It was not until our sixth session that the breakthrough came.

Phillip came into my room beaming all over his face, saying proudly, even before he sat down, 'Robert, I've remembered something at last. It was something you said last time, about Grandpa, father's father. It's all come back. It happened when I was about 11.'

'What happened?' I asked.

'When we were young, we used to stay with Grandpa a lot. I told you last time that I don't care for him, and try not to see much of him. It was my birthday the day before yesterday, and Grannie sent me a fiver, and I was thinking about it in bed, and it all came back in a flash.

'Grandpa is what I suppose you would call a gentleman farmer. He's never done much work himself, if any, but he has quite a large farm, and we always used to stay with them sometime during the school holidays.

'One day I said to him – when I was about 11, as I've said – that I would like to learn to drive a car, and he said, why not? Naturally, I couldn't learn on the public roads, but there was nothing illegal about my learning on the private roads of the farm.

'I was tall for my age, but even so, I remember that I had a lot of difficulty reaching the pedals. Grandpa had wooden blocks fixed to them, and I got on quite well. He took me out every day, and I couldn't wait for him to call me for a lesson.

'Then one day, while I was driving, he undid my flies and took out my cock and began to play with it. I was horrified.'

'Did you get an erection?' I asked.

'Yes. That was one of the horrible things about it. I knew it was wrong somehow for him to be doing this to me, and I was making it easier for him by getting a hard-on.'

'So, what did you do?' I asked.

'I quickly stopped the van, jumped out and ran home. When I got home, my sister Elizabeth met me and asked, "Whatever are you doing with your cock hanging out of your shorts?" That was more embarrassing still. I didn't answer, but I stopped long enough to push my cock back into my shorts, brushed past her and ran up to my room.

'In a minute or two, Grandpa came up to my room. He was very agitated and began to cry. "Please forgive me," he said. "I shouldn't have done that. Please never tell anyone about it, will you? Please promise me! Look, here's a fiver."

'I pushed away his hand holding the money. It was Grannie's fiver that brought it all back.' Phillip smiled at me. 'Wasn't I daft? I could have taken him for a bomb.'

'No, you couldn't,' I told him. 'You're much too decent to blackmail an old man.'

'You're quite right,' he said. 'I couldn't have done it. Why haven't I remembered it until now?'

'Because it was a horrible experience, and you wanted to forget it, and did so very effectively,' I replied, then had to explain to him how traumas can be pushed right to the bottom of the memory, if they are bad enough. I went on, 'I think you ought to know that something happens to some men when they get old which makes them behave in that way. Do your grandparents sleep together?'

'No, they have separate rooms.'

'That could explain it all. Even seven or eight years ago, it's possible that your grandmother had gone off sex. Some women do as they get older, and their partners get thrown out of sexual balance, which makes them do the sort of things that Grandpa did to you. It could quite well have happened to your sister.'

'I hadn't thought of that.'

'Try to be sympathetic,' I urged him. 'Thwarted old men can be very unhappy. On the other hand, they should do all they can to control themselves. Since you've remembered all this, have you tried to masturbate?'

'Yes – twice!'

'And?'

'No change.'

'We must see what we can do for you.'

'What can you do?'

'I, personally, can't do anything, because I have a rule never to get physically involved with my patients. But I would like you to meet George, because he, I think, would be less threatening, until we've got you working properly, than Sylvia. One of your chief worries has been that you can't share in your friends' intimacies. When George has put you right, as a reward we'll give you the chance of proving yourself to Sylvia.'

I explained who George was and, after a moment or two's thought, he agreed.

'There won't be a miracle, unless I'm very much mistaken,' I warned him. 'You'll have to be patient. I believe everything will come all right once you get to know George well.'

It took George four sessions to effect a full cure. It is

impossible to describe the happy relief with which Phillip glowed the first time it happened. He actually wept when it happened the second time. I sent Sylvia in to him to console him.

A few months ago I had a letter from his girl-friend, saying she could not control him sexually. He was wearing her out. He had told her his history, so she was not complaining. All she asked was, 'Is he normal?'

To which I replied, 'You couldn't find a more normal young man. Enjoy him!'

9 Help!

TWO DAYS before Christmas four or five years ago, I was just sitting down to dinner at home – it was 8.00 p.m., I suppose – when my telephone rang. L. was busy with last-minute preparations, so I went to the phone myself, and when I said my number, I heard a weeping woman's voice asking, 'Is that Dr Chartham?' I said it was, and then asked, 'Who gave you my number?'

My home telephone number has always been ex-directory, so that I should not be troubled by people ringing up when I was relaxing. I felt somewhat annoyed, therefore, by being disturbed by this unknown woman, and on the point of telling her to get in touch with the Samaritans, when she named one of the Samaritans' own therapists.

As I have explained earlier, I used to work closely with the Samaritans at this time. I would take their clients who were the victims of one of my specialities, and in return they would accept my patients whose problems were not entirely sexual, as they did in the case of my 'favourite shoplifter'. I knew that John would not have given the caller my private number, especially at this time in the evening, if he had not been convinced that I could help her better than any of his local Samaritans.

'Do you know John?' I asked her.

'No,' she said. 'I only rang the Samaritans a few minutes ago, and he took my call. He said he was sure you would be able to help me.'

'What's the trouble?' I enquired.

'The police have just arrested my husband and the social workers have taken my children into care,' she wept.

'For God's sake, why?' I exclaimed. It seemed a heartlessly cruel thing to do, to take children from their mother

and their home and put them in an institution, just two days before Christmas.

'I'd rather not say over the telephone,' she said. 'I know I'm asking a great deal, Dr Chartham, but could you possibly come here. I daren't come to you in case my husband rings.'

'Where do you live?'

She told me. It was a desolate spot in the depths of the county, about 25 kilometres away.

'I'll have a bite to eat,' I told her. 'I've had a heavy day and I'm hungry, and I'll be with you in about three-quarters of an hour.'

'I am so sorry to put you to all this trouble, but it is very serious,' she apologised.

'If John told you to ring me, that's good enough for me,' I assured her.

The house, which I found after a little difficulty, stood alone, well back from the road. For a country road, it was quite wide, but a couple of hundred metres to the east there was a long bend, sharp enough to be dangerous for traffic going over 80 kilometres an hour. I recalled that, despite the warning signs, there had been several accidents at this spot.

I reversed into the drive, and walked up to the house. In response to my knock, a woman's voice called from the other side of the door, 'Who is it?'

'Robert Chartham.'

As she closed the door behind me, she said, 'My name is Anne X. It is very kind of you to come like this. Come into the sitting-room.'

I took off my overcoat and placed it on a chair in the hall, and followed her into the room.

Taking my first good look at her, I saw that under the strain of whatever had happened, she was a beautiful woman, probably in her early 30s. On the mantelpiece I noticed pictures of two young children, which, if recent, showed a boy of about ten and a girl of seven or eight. There was a family snapshot, too, of a good-looking man, giving the impression of being kind and gentle, whom I

presumed to be the father. He was a year or two older than Anne, by appearance.

'Have you any scotch?' I asked. 'Because if you have, I'd like a tot, and you must have one, too.'

'We don't drink much,' she said, 'but we keep a bottle in for friends.'

She went to a cupboard in a corner and took out a bottle and two glasses. Putting them on a small table beside me, she said, 'Will you pour them out? I'm not very good at it. Andrew always does it. Would you like soda?'

'No, thanks,' I told her. 'And I think you should have yours neat, too.'

She smiled faintly for the first time. 'I'll get tight.'

'I don't think you will,' I smiled back. 'Now, what's the trouble?'

She looked into the fire for a minute or two, saying eventually, 'Samaritan John says you are the most understanding man he knows and quite unshockable.'

'I'm not sure about the first, but the second is possible,' I said. 'Try me!'

I don't know what I was expecting to hear, but something pretty horrific, so I felt a bit let down when she said, 'My husband is a cross-dresser.'

'So?' I said. 'My file on transvestites is half-full of cross-dressing husbands. Is he homosexual, too, and has got into trouble for soliciting?'

'No, nothing like that. He has weak homosexual tendencies. He sleeps with his oldest friend about once a year. The friend is totally homosexual, but very nice. Andrew always tells me when they have made love.'

'Do you mind?'

'I have little pangs of regret that I can't satisfy him fully, but not enough to upset our relationship.'

'How did you discover that Andrew cross-dressed?' I asked.

'He told me when he proposed to me.'

'That was honest of him,' I remarked.

'He is an entirely honest man, and gentle and kind and loving.'

'What was your reaction?'

'Surprise! But I didn't feel disgusted or shocked. You see, I was absolutely in love with him.'

'And still are?'

'Utterly! I just can't understand why they have done this to us.'

'Have you ever suggested that he should have treatment?'

'It's never occurred to me. He only dresses at home, and then not more than two or three times a month. When he does, he's much more passionate than usually, and I like that. So why bother to change him? Is it possible?'

'I personally don't believe so, and when you have a relationship like yours, I don't think it's even necessary to try, unless there are children, who might create a problem. What about your children?'

'A boy, Robert, and a girl, Sandra.' Her lips quivered as she spoke and her eyes filled with tears.

'Do they know about their father?'

She nodded, sipped her whisky and said, 'We thought it best to tell them when they asked.'

'When did you tell them?'

'About eighteen months ago.'

'What did you tell them?'

'That daddy liked playing a dressing-up game now and again.'

'Had he dressed in their presence before they asked?' I enquired. 'I'm sorry. He must have done, otherwise they wouldn't have asked.'

'He tried not to dress until they had gone to bed, or were out. But, I'll admit, they did catch a glimpse of him now and again.'

'But they said nothing?' She shook her head. 'Did something particular happen to make them ask?'

'Yes. We've always told them they mustn't come into our bedroom without knocking. One day they went to the cinema, and got over-excited by something they saw there. We didn't hear them come home. We were in the bedroom. They couldn't find us so decided we must be upstairs, and in

their excitement they burst into the bedroom without knocking.'

'And?'

'Andrew was dressing, and I was helping him with his bra . . .'

'You help him dress?'

'Oh, yes! I help him choose his clothes quite often. We hadn't expected the children to be home so early, and Andrew had a really strong urge. It was during the school holidays – Andrew is a schoolmaster. We had intended to make love as soon as he was dressed, but we didn't have time. We were rather cross with the children and, in any case, Andrew being so turned on had turned me on, too. So we sent them away, and made love quickly. We both felt awful about being angry with them, so tried to make up by being specially nice. Over tea, Robert asked the question.'

'Weren't you afraid they would tell their friends?'

'No. We explained that not all daddies want to dress up, and that a lot of people think that those who do are a bit funny, so it would be best for all of us if we kept daddy's dressing up a family secret.'

'And there are no better guardians of secrets than children,' I smiled.

'Absolutely right,' she replied. 'After a while, Andrew used to dress while the children were about and come downstairs. Not very often, but we didn't want them to think that we were ashamed of what he did. Now and again there were one or two searching questions, but we answered them honestly and as well as we could and they seemed to understand.'

'And now something has happened,' I said.

'Yes,' she said, then added hurriedly, 'but not through any fault of the children.'

'Tell me,' I coaxed her.

They had sat down to tea about four o'clock. Andrew had 'dressed'. (He always had a very strong urge to do so towards the end of the month – a point which I have always intended to research but have never found time.) They

were all happy; there was already a feeling of Christmas surrounding them, Anne said.

Then all of a sudden there was a terrible crash outside.

Jumping up, Andrew had exclaimed, 'Another accident! Phone the police and the ambulance, Anne, and I'll go and see what has happened. Children, you are not to leave the house!'

Then, completely forgetting that he was 'dressed', Andrew had rushed out of the house. When she had telephoned the police and the ambulance, Anne had joined him. Some of the car-lights were still working, and in their light one could see a scene of absolute carnage.

A mini-bus carrying some old-age pensioners, returning from a Christmas party in a village not far away, had crashed into a huge Mercedes driven by a young man who lay dead, pinned to the steering column; a friend sitting beside him, almost guillotined by the windscreen, was also dead, but in the back was a third, unconscious but still living boy.

The mini-bus had run off the road into the ditch and lay tilting over to one side. The driver was dead, and so were two of his elderly passengers. Two others were unhurt, except for shock, but another was bleeding profusely from the mouth.

'We did what we could for them, comforting the old people who were not hurt, and trying to staunch the bleeding of the boy in the back of the Merc, and whatever else we could think of doing,' Anne told me.

Fortunately, the ambulance and police arrived on the scene very quickly, and Andrew, still 'dressed', and Anne were tending to the injured when they did. The police radioed for another ambulance to take away the dead, while the living were rushed to hospital in the first.

'The police inspector left a sergeant and two constables – I think – to write their reports and get the motors removed,' Anne said, 'and, with another sergeant, came to the house with us. When he asked Andrew his name, and Andrew told him, I saw the sergeant look at him sharply, but neither he nor the inspector said anything.

'They took down our statements. They must have been with us at least three-quarters of an hour. They questioned Robert and Sandra briefly. I recall Sandra saying, "We heard a crash, Daddy jumped up and told Mummy to phone the police and ambulance and told us not to leave the house, and then he went out." They thanked us for our help and said that, if they needed our help over any point, they would come back. But they still said nothing as they left.'

As soon as the police had left, Andrew went upstairs to change, followed by Anne, and they discussed what might happen.

'Andrew was depressed,' Anne told me, 'but I believed that, as they hadn't said anything, in the circumstances they would overlook it, or at most give Andrew a warning.'

She could not have been more wrong. The police did return an hour and a half later, not to warn Andrew but to arrest him on a charge of 'being in a public place, to wit, Her Majesty's highway, in female clothing, in circumstances likely to cause a breach of Her Majesty's peace.'

That was bad enough, but worse was to follow.

The police had brought with them social workers, and the social workers had obtained a warrant to take the two children into care. Their grounds for this action were that Andrew and his aberration were in danger of corrupting Robert's and Sandra's morals.

When Anne finished her account, quite naturally she was in tears again, and I was so stunned by the ruthlessness of the police that I sat like a block of wood, unable to move.

Anne brought me back to reality, asking, 'What are we going to do, Dr Chartham? Is there anything we can do?'

'There is a lot we can do,' I told her. 'Have you spoken with your solicitor?'

'We haven't one,' she said.

'I have one who is a friend. May I use your phone?'

I telephoned the friend, and explained the situation to him. He agreed to be in court the following morning. He would advise Andrew to exercise his rights to be tried by

jury in the Crown Court. In this way he would have an opportunity to organise a defence, be legally represented and, with any luck, get bail.

'What do you mean – "with any luck get bail"?' I asked.

'He might get remanded in custody,' he said. 'Our magistrates are such fuddy-duddies, they might panic when a case like this comes before them. By the way, am I right in thinking you know Foster-Penrose?' David Foster-Penrose was the Chief Constable of our county police.

'I do, as a matter of fact,' I said. 'Fairly well. He calls me in as expert witness sometimes.'

'I thought I heard that you give evidence for the fuzz,' he said, surprising me by his irreverent description of the police. 'Do you think you could have a word with him, and explain what's happened and ask him if he could possibly instruct his chaps not to oppose bail tomorrow morning? Just to be on the safe side! It would be improper for me to do so, but if you know Foster-Penrose fairly well, he won't clap you in irons even if he does refuse.'

'I'll try,' I said. 'What about the children?'

'That's much more difficult. We'll need to get an order from a High Court judge "in chambers" to get them out of care.'

'Before Christmas?'

'We'll have a damn good try. Ring me back when you've spoken to F-P.'

I rang county police HQ to be told that the Chief Constable was at his home. Luckily I had his private telephone number in my diary. He was not happy at being dragged away from the TV.

'It's *Starsky and Hutch*,' he complained. 'I like a good laugh at someone else's expense. What can I do for you, doctor?'

I told him, and he listened graciously and patiently. When I had finished, he asked, 'Who'll stand bail for him?'

On the spur of the moment I said I would, and I imagined his wife would, too.

'If you're a surety,' he said flatteringly, 'that's good enough for me.'

I thanked him sincerely, and rang off to dial my lawyer friend.

'Good,' he said dryly. 'We'll have to go to the High Court in London to find a judge in chambers. I'll get my clerk to set the wheels in motion while we're in court tomorrow morning. See you then.'

The proceedings in court took only a few minutes. I thought the magistrates looked relieved when my friend stood up and said, 'My client elects to go to trial, sir.'

'Very well,' said the chairman of the bench.

'I apply for bail,' my friend went on.

Before the chairman could say anything, the police superintendent conducting the police case, jumped up and said, 'We do not oppose bail, sir.'

The magistrates whispered among themselves for a couple of minutes, then the chairman said, clearing his throat, 'Two sureties of £500 each.'

My friend said, 'The defendant's wife and Dr Robert Chartham are prepared to be bound over in those sums, sir.'

'Very well,' said the chairman. 'Case remitted to the Crown Court . . . Next case.'

As my friend had said, it was not so easy to get the children out of care, and it was after four o'clock when a judge signed the order for their release. While we were waiting for the document to be prepared, the judge arranged for tea to be brought, and asked Anne to pour.

As he munched on a biscuit, the old man said to Andrew, 'Never met one of you chaps before. Wish we had time for a chat. You look normal enough.'

And as we left, 'Forget all about this over Christmas. Have a happy time, for the children's sake.'

But how could there be a happy Christmas for them when the atmosphere was artificial as pretence must be?

We collected the two frightened children as soon as we could. Even the short time they had spent in the institution had had a devastating effect on them.

At his subsequent trial, Andrew was found guilty, but given a suspended sentence. Nevertheless he lost his job.

But what was really incomprehensible to me was that the children were placed in care again, and this time it took us several months to get them out. This time they had been separated, and I believe they have both been scarred for life by a stupid bureaucracy.

Man's inhumanity to man!

10 'Jim, What Are You Doing to Our Ethel?'

JIM AND Ethel were approaching their late 20s when they came to see me.

They came into my consulting-room nervously, even apprehensively, and the thanks they gave Sylvia, when she had briefly introduced me, was wan.

Usually, when a couple ask me to help them with a problem affecting their relationship, and they visit me together, I see them separately to begin with. I do this because it is an odd but true fact that the presence of a partner prevents very many people from giving a full version of the problem from their own point of view. They seem unable fully to unburden themselves because, I believe, they think that their partner will consider that something they feel is an expression of disloyalty. Yet it is vital for the therapist to become aware of attitudes towards the partner, because these attitudes, more often than not, represent a constituent of the problem which is making both of them miserable. The really experienced psychologist is able to apportion more correctly the responsibility for the problem if he knows *all* that is in the mind of each, and by co-relating both accounts, can make a more exact diagnosis and prescribe a treatment.

If this should appear to the reader to be as clear as mud, let me put it more simply, if more crudely. Very often a man or a woman will not give a full version of their own 'side' of a problem in the presence of the partner. Even if during their sole interview with the therapist, they lie by imputing blame to the other partner or withholding their own role in the relationship, it is essential for the therapist to know exactly what each thinks.

I base my counselling on this arrangement. Only when I

have seen each on his/her own, do I see them together. Thus, when forming my diagnosis, I have three versions on which to work.

I explained all this as tactfully as I could to Jim and Ethel, and asked who would like to be interviewed first.

'I think, in our case, Dr Chartham,' Jim said, 'that it would be a waste of all our time if you saw us separately, because, you see, neither of us is blaming the other for what is happening to us. We have read some of your books, and we realise that I have been psychologically affected in such a way as to cause this problem.'

'Oh!' I said. This was a fairly unusual approach. 'Tell me,' I went on, 'why do you think that you, Jim, have a problem which has psychological causes and why do you agree with Jim, Ethel?'

'Well,' said Ethel. 'The basic problem is a very simple one. When we try to make love now, Jim can't get an erection, no matter what I do to help him . . .'

'And she's very skilful, too,' Jim put in.

'We always thought that if we *knew* why we had a problem like ours, it would automatically right itself. But it hasn't, even after some months, though we've tried everything we can think of that might help.'

'Ethel's right,' Jim said. 'We have tried everything, and because there's absolutely no sign of a change for the better, we're getting so desperate, we have come to see you.'

'All right!' I said. 'Let's start at the beginning. You're married! How long?'

'About five months,' Jim said.

'Five months and two-and-a-half weeks,' Ethel said, more precisely.

Jim was an accountant and Ethel was personal assistant to Jim's boss. They had first got to know one another on a more intimate footing after an office party, at which Jim had made a tentative play for Ethel, which she had not rejected. By degrees they had settled down to going steady and had presently decided that, as it seemed likely that they might eventually marry unless something unforeseen hap-

pened to change their minds, there was no reason why they should not make love. Soon they were doing so twice a week (sometimes more often) at Jim's flat – Ethel lived with her parents – with a long weekend once a month, when they stayed at the flat of a divorced friend of Jim's.

'Though we were both virgins,' Ethel said, 'everything went well from the word go. But we realised that we could be missing out quite a lot, so Jim bought a copy of your book *The Sensuous Couple*. In fact, as soon as we began to use some of your suggestions, we knew we were.'

'Then your *Sex Manners for Advanced Lovers* taught us quite a lot more,' Jim added.

For two or three years they were satisfied and happy, sexually and emotionally. Then they began to think about having a family, and this meant marriage.

'We're not so selfish that we could deprive any children we might have of the security which only a happy family life can provide. At least, that is how we think,' Ethel said.

So they decided to get married. They looked around for somewhere to live and found a house, in a small development of a dozen junior-executive-type houses, still in the process of being built. The builder gave them a completion date, and they arranged to be married a month after that date.

'As the weeks passed and the completion date came nearer, we did begin to get a bit apprehensive about the slow progress they were making on the house. However, the builder assured us again and again, with his hand on his heart, that it would be finished in time,' Jim said.

'Then the awful thing happened!' Ethel said.

'And what was that?' I asked.

'Two weeks after we had sent out all the wedding invitations, we heard that the builder had gone bankrupt!' Jim exclaimed.

'He didn't even have the face to come and tell us, either,' Ethel put in. 'He left us to hear about it through gossip.'

'So what did you do?' I asked.

'Ethel's pa was marvellous,' Jim said. 'He went out of his

way to find another builder. Obviously, it's going to cost us more than the original price . . .'

'But we don't mind that. It's such a lovely position and the house itself – four bedrooms – is just right for a junior executive,' Ethel remarked.

'But I don't see what the problem can be,' I told them, wishing they would get on with their story a bit faster.

'Well,' Jim explained, 'the new builder couldn't finish in time for us to furnish it before the wedding and move into it when we came back from our honeymoon.'

'After a lot of talk, we decided we must go on with the wedding as planned rather than put everyone off. Some of my mother's relations were coming from Scotland and had made their arrangements.'

'Unfortunately,' said Jim, 'I'd sold the lease of my flat and couldn't go back on the sale, otherwise we could have lived there until the house was ready. Anyhow, Ethel's parents had quite a big house, and they suggested we should live with them for the time being.'

'Not the best of arrangements,' I commented, beginning to think I might know the cause of their – or at least Jim's – problem; were they, or at least was he, inhibited from making love freely in case they should be overheard by Ethel's parents?

'We realised that,' said Ethel, 'but it was only going to be for a few weeks . . .'

'We hoped,' put in Jim, with a wry smile.

'And it's spun out to five months?' I said.

'Yes,' Jim went on, 'and it's likely to stretch out to three or four months more. And, from every point of view except the one we've mentioned, we're getting on very well.'

'No in-law trouble?' I said.

'No!' they both said.

'Then what?'

It had been a Sunday morning and the house was quiet as most of its occupants were enjoying the traditional 'lie-in'.

Ethel and Jim had been to a party at the house of some friends. They were still waking up when Ethel's father

brought their early-morning tea, his sole contribution to the domestic chores.

'Your mother deserves a lie-in once a week,' he used to remark solemnly, not appreciating the irony of what he was saying.

'Have a good party?' he asked as he put the tray down on the bedside table.

Rousing himself, and propping himself up on an elbow, Jim said, 'Yes, thanks!' and was vaguely aware of a movement in the doorway beyond his father-in-law.

'Don't you get cold sleeping raw?' Ethel's father asked.

'No!' Jim said, slightly resenting being forced awake so quickly.

'Maybe I'll try it some time!' the older man commented, 'if I can get Ethel's ma to come round to it.'

'Yes,' Jim commented.

'Well! Drink your tea before it gets cold,' said Mr Brown, and backed out of the room.

'Goodness! I thought he was never going!' Ethel said sleepily, as the door closed. 'I can do with a drink. My mouth is all dry! Drank too much.'

She half sat up to take the cup which Jim was passing to her, and the action brought her beautiful breasts into full view above the bed-clothes. Jim felt the movement of response throb inside him and move up his penis from its very root imbedded in his belly up to its roundly pointed tip. He leaned over and closed his lips round the nearest nipple, which hardened at once to the caress of his lips and tongue.

'Watch out!' Ethel warned him with a little laugh, as the cup moved with a tinkle in the unsteady saucer. 'You'll make me spill my tea.'

Jim withdrew his mouth, planting a kiss on her up-tilted breast as he did so. Side by side they lay, propped up, and drank their tea, chatting, still not quite wide awake, about the party.

When she had finished her tea, she handed her cup and saucer back to Jim, who put it on the small table on his side of the bed, beside his own, then she snuggled down beside

him with a contented sigh. He turned on his side towards her, and putting an arm round her, pulled her gently towards him, until he could feel the sharp points of her roused nipples pricking his chest, and the sensitive tip of his penis, engorged with desire, stimulating itself against the abrasiveness of her pubic bush.

With welling contentment, they caressed and stroked, tongue jabbing tongue, lips drawing searing moisture from the other's mouth, muscles growing taut and relaxing whenever the nerves of sex contacted them. Sounds of mounting vocalising synchronised with the rising sensations of climax coming from both of them masked the noise of passing cars and the clatter of the milk-crates being delivered along the street, filling the room.

Urgently, her pelvis arching upwards, Ethel said, 'Come in me, darling! Please, please! Quickly!'

Jim drew away from her momentarily, the better to raise himself to mount her. With a deft movement, he covered her body with the length of his, aware of his throbbing penis crushed between his pubis and hers and, almost at once, of her hands insinuating themselves between their bellies. He arched his buttocks and felt her fingers gently seize his penis and firmly guide it to the swollen entrance of her secret interior, and, thrusting forward and upward, was enveloped in a scabbard of incredible warmth, which sent a glow of demanding desire through his loins and opened upwards and outwards and downwards.

Automatically the movements of love took over both their bodies and their senses, and with each thrust and retreat, each meeting and withdrawal, they became more and more oblivious of everything but the welling of their rapidly approaching private crises. And as their climaxes came inexorably nearer, so their ears became full of their own sounds of urgent delight.

As both passed the point-of-no-return, they were enveloped in a world of delicious magic, and then as they gave the final greeting to the apex of their loving, the magic was broken by a small piping voice saying above them, 'What are you doing to our Ethel, Jim?'

'It was just like a hit on the back of the head with a hammer,' Jim said.

'It was my 11-year-old brother, Francis,' Ethel explained.

'I'd seen him vaguely out on the landing through the open door when father-in-law brought in the tea, but he'd never been in our room before when we were there,' Jim went on. 'My cock went completely limp in a second, and I rolled off Ethel . . .'

'And I screamed at the little horror to go away,' said Ethel. 'Well, Dad and Mum heard me, and Francis was scared and ran out of the room straight into Dad's arms.'

'Pa-in-law had realised what must have happened,' Jim grinned, 'and gave the kid a resounding clip over the head, and bundled him into his room. When we met at breakfast later it was all a bit uncomfortable. Ma-in-law said, "Well, you do make a bit of a carry on, you know. No wonder the poor lad wondered what was going on!" "That was no reason for the brat to go sneaking into their room, mother!" said pa-in-law. "I've been telling you for months you ought to have a word with him about sex," mother-in-law retorted. "When have I had the time? You've got to choose the right moment, you know. You just can't take him by the ear and say . . ." and so it went on.'

'It had been a bit of a shock,' Ethel said. 'Poor Jim was shaking from head to foot for quite a time.'

'You were . . .' Jim began.

Sensing they might start to bicker a little, I said, 'I can understand exactly what your reactions were. They were perfectly natural. So what happened afterwards?'

'Well, I was still wanting to come off,' Ethel replied, 'so I asked Jim to come in me again.'

'But I'd come just as the boy spoke, and I didn't feel like it again so soon after, so I did the next best thing,' Jim remarked. 'It was only that night that we discovered the worst.'

'Which was?' I asked, though I thought I knew what he would say.

'When we tried to make love again, as soon as I got inside Ethel, I went soft,' he said.

'And it happens every time now, even though you lock the door?' I suggested.

'Yes,' Ethel agreed, surprise in her voice. 'We thought it would be all right if we locked the door. We could understand what had happened and why, but surely it should have come right if we could stop it from happening again?'

'And it hasn't?' I commented.

'No,' said Jim. 'And another thing is that, because of what Ethel's mother said about our making a noise, we are so self-conscious now when we make love it's having a terrible effect on our responses. Neither of us has been *really* satisfied, whatever we have tried as an alternative to actual fucking.'

'When are you going to be able to move into your house?' I asked.

'Another couple of months or so,' Ethel replied. 'It's all getting a bit too much. What can we do? There must be something, for heaven's sake!'

'The only thing that will put things right,' I said, 'will be for you to stop sleeping in that room. You see, I believe that it's not only *what* happened, but *where* it happened, too, that is contributing to your problem. I'm not absolutely certain that I am right, but I feel pretty sure I am. It's the old, old story of psychological responses to an event or certain surroundings blocking physical responses. You must do something to break the pattern, and since you've made sure the event cannot happen again, by locking your bedroom door, the only thing which will break the pattern is different surroundings. Have you friends with whom you could stay for a long weekend, for example?'

'My brother and his wife are always asking us to have a weekend with them,' Jim said. He smiled across at Ethel. 'There are no kids there yet.'

'May I suggest you get in touch with them as soon as possible?' I said. 'Let me know how you get on.'

Ten days or so later, Jim telephoned me.

'It worked,' he said. 'It was wonderful to be able to have it away properly again. But . . .'

'But it's all happening again now that you've returned to Ethel's parents?' I asked.

'Exactly!' he said. 'What are we going to do?'

'Well,' I told him, 'you know that you can overcome your problem. You've either got to make the best of what you are able to do with each other until you can move into your own house, or, if you can't wait for that, rent a furnished place.'

'I see!' he said. 'Well, thanks, anyhow!'

I don't know what they did. Some keep in touch. Some don't!

11 'I Know, He Does Look a Bit of a Berk'

It sometimes happened, though very infrequently, that Sylvia would leave to go to the shops towards the end of the afternoon, before my last 'patient' of the day arrived, and I had to answer the door myself. On one of these occasions, when I opened the door I found myself confronted by a very pretty young woman, whom I put in her early 20s, accompanied by a rather scruffy boy, with an afro hair-do, wearing patched denim and no tie, but with a wonderful smile and sparkling eyes.

Despite the contrast in their appearance, I took them to be husband and wife. Sylvia's note had said that the wife, Janet, had written, begging for a consultation, and as quite often a *couple* would appear at the clinic, perhaps I may be forgiven for having made a mistake.

I asked them into the waiting-room.

'OK,' I said. 'When a couple come to see me I see them separately to begin with. Who's coming first?'

The girl cottoned on at once.

With a delicious ripple of laughter, she exclaimed, 'This isn't David, my husband. This is a friend, Harry! He's just come along to keep me company.'

'Well, Harry,' I said. 'Make yourself comfortable here, while I have a word with Janet.'

In the consulting-room, before I could tell her to sit down, she burst into a ripple of infectious laughter.

'I know!' she giggled. 'He does look a bit of a berk, doesn't he? But under those patched, scruffy jeans is a cock that has magic in it – at least as far as I'm concerned.'

Motioning her to the chair facing the desk, I said tritely,

'It never does to go by appearances. Now what's your difficulty?'

She took a packet of cigarettes from her handbag after rummaging in it for some seconds. 'Do you mind?' she asked.

I did mind. Since I gave up smoking a dozen years ago, I cannot abide other peoples' cigarette smoke. On the other hand, I do appreciate the ordeal which telling the most intimate details of their personal sex-lives to a stranger represents to many people, and that a cigarette can have a calming effect in such circumstances, so I said, 'Go ahead!' and went over to the windows and switched on the twin expel fans.

She lit up and took a long drag.

'Funny, isn't it?' she said. 'Ever since I got your letter giving me an appointment, I've been looking forward to talking to you, but now you're there, sitting on the other side of this desk, I'm nearly wetting my panties with nerves.'

'It often happens,' I tried to reassure her. 'Take your time, Janet. How old are you?'

'Nineteen,' she said.

'How long have you been married?'

'Three years.'

She 'saw' me doing a quick mental sum.

'You're quite right. We got married a fortnight after my sixteenth birthday.'

'How old is David?'

'Twenty-one.'

'Any children?'

'One boy.'

'Age?'

'Three years two months!' she replied, in a tone, and with a look of defiance.

'I'm not commenting!' I said. 'Is the boy the cause of what has gone wrong?'

'Martin? Good God no!' she laughed. 'You can do sums in your head very well, can't you?'

'I wasn't much good at mental arithmetic at school,' I

told her, and added, 'Like to tell me all about it?'

'Of course!' she said, and stubbed out her cigarette and lit another.

She and David had met at a school disco. He was a tall, dark and wildly handsome sixth-former, aged 17, and she was a – very pretty, I imagine – 15-year-old member of the lower sixth.

'I've always been rather a randy lady,' she said. 'I began rubbing myself off before I was ten. I think I must have been physically precocious because I found orgasm – I climax during intercourse without difficulty, and have multi-orgasms three times out of five – so fantastic from the word go that I went a bit mad until I was about 14.'

'When did you begin to menstruate?' I asked.

'Two or three months before I was 12, and I had a reasonably thick pubic bush by the time I was 13.'

'What about your bosom?'

'Funnily enough, my boobs had only swelled just a little bit by then, but my nipples were very sensitive, and the first time I went to bed with my best friend Alice – she was a few months older than me, but had older brothers and sisters, and knew all the physical facts about the birds and the bees – and had my nipples played with for the first time, I found I could climax just by touching them up and not doing anything else.'

It seemed that she was quite a sexually responsive girl, but although she was interested in boys, and found that she was quite attractive to a good many, she never got past the light-petting stage with them.

'David's was the first cock I ever held, though I had seen my brother-in-law with a hard-on when I was staying with him and my sister and burst in on him in the bathroom one morning. That doesn't mean to say, though, that I didn't often wonder what it would be like to have a cock in me.'

'Weren't you ever tempted physically to get into deep petting?' I suggested.

'A few times, maybe. A lot of times I got turned on, but I guess I must be a fussy girl,' she stubbed out her cigarette

and grinned, 'though you wouldn't think so, having seen Harry, would you?'

'There may be good psycho-sexual reasons why you accept Harry as a lover,' I told her.

'You're right!' she said. 'I think – I know this is silly – that it was because most of the boys who got me into a corner weren't particularly careful about the cleanliness of their hands, and specially their finger-nails. One or two, even when otherwise attractive, had a kind of musty smell about them which put me off. David says uncircumcised boys who aren't too fussy about washing under their foreskins often smell like that.'

David was quite different from any boy who had previously made a pass at her. He was neat in his appearance, scrupulously clean, and, in her judgement, really handsome.

He had seen her home from the disco. 'And he actually asked me if he could kiss me goodnight! I'd have been totally mortified if he hadn't! He kissed quite passionately but kept his hands to himself.'

A few days later, he asked her to go to the cinema with him. They held hands most of the time, and it wasn't until nearly the end that he put an arm round her and a hand over one of her breasts.

'I came just by his rubbing his thumb lightly over my dress! I felt rather ashamed. Dr Chartham, do you think girls of 14 and 15 can really fall in love?'

'I think it depends,' I said.

'On what?'

'On how psychologically mature they are. Love is a mixture of physical attraction and emotional response. Personally I don't see why, in certain circumstances, a young girl shouldn't feel emotionally in love with a boy. When you are young, physical response to a high degree of sexual satisfaction is easy. But in an on-going relationship, eventually physical satisfaction is not enough. That is why, I think, that the young tend to be more promiscuous than the more mature.'

'From that first kiss,' she went on, 'there was no other

boy for me but David. It wasn't infatuation, I assure you. I couldn't imagine what life would be without him. It wasn't the physical thing either, because it was only on our sixth or seventh time out together that we got into petting. From my point of view, that first sort of semi-petting was fantastic. David said that it was for him, too. He'd done it with boys, whom he liked very much, but he'd never come off with such a thrill, as the first time I did it for him. That made me very happy, and it was the kind of happiness that only real love can – er – produce. Having it away with Harry is marvellous, but I don't feel for him what I felt and still feel for David, in spite of everything. I'll tell you all about Harry in a minute.'

After that first time, heavy petting became more and more frequent. David revealed that he had a sex-drive that matched Janet's, and they often petted three or four times in the course of an evening together. But there was always something, some little thing that prevented them from achieving 100 per cent ecstasy.

'I think we both knew what it was. I ached to have him in me, and he ached to come in me. I wouldn't have raised a finger to stop him, but he never made any move. Then once when we were talking he said that, apart from the fact that I wasn't on the Pill and he hadn't any french letters, when we did go all the way, he wanted everything to be absolutely right. Not in the back of the car, or in the corner of a field where someone might come along and spoil it, or fully clothed on his Mum's settee, but naked in a soft bed, and no one about to interrupt.'

Janet wanted it to be that way, too, so she didn't argue with him, but both did their best to make their stimulating techniques more sophisticated.

'Your books helped us a lot, Dr Chartham, especially *Sex Manners for Advanced Lovers* which got us into oral, and *The Sensuous Couple* which made it even better.'

So they courted for months and Janet took her 'O' levels and David his 'A' levels, which he hoped would get him a place at a polytechnic, where he could learn computer programming and kindred subjects. They made no secret of

their love affair from their parents and, in fact, received the latter's tacit approval.

'His dad did take him to one side once, and told him not to get too ardent – lovely word that, isn't it? – because I was under 16 and there would be trouble if anything happened. My mum and dad liked him so much and so did my older sister, that I don't think that any of them gave a thought to the possibility that we might have it away.'

An opportunity for them to satisfy their criteria for the *mise-en-scène* for their first complete lovemaking occurred during the summer holidays following their examinations. David's parents had arranged to go to Italy for a holiday, and as David had been lucky enough to get a holiday job, he couldn't go with them. He was quite capable of looking after himself – he was a good cook – and Janet's mother had promised his mother that she would see to it that he did not starve, and Janet, for her part, undertook to keep the house in order.

'Neither of our parents seemed to be at all suspicious of what we might get up to.'

David's parents left for Italy on a Saturday morning. David had Saturdays off, and he and Janet went with them to the airport. In the afternoon they played tennis with friends, and afterwards they all went to David's house for a cup of tea. Then the friends left.

'As he shut the front door after them, David suddenly raised his right arm, lowered his nose and sniffed,' Janet told me. ' "I need a shower," he said. "What about you, Jan?" I swear, Dr Chartham, that when I said a shower would be nice, I had no idea what was going to happen. Mind you, I don't think it would have stopped me from going upstairs with him, if I had had any idea.

'He stripped off in seconds. It was the first time I had seen him completely naked, and he looked infinitely more handsome than I had ever believed him to be. I remember every detail of that first time we were really alone together. He moved quickly to me, kissed me deeply, then pecked at one of my nipples with his lips. Then he was gone and next minute I heard the hissing of the shower. I undressed

quickly, and when I was naked, I caught a quick glance in a long mirror and saw that my labia were swollen, and I could feel them throbbing.

'When I went into the bathroom I saw that David already had a full erection. It was silly really, because although I had played with his cock during our petting sessions, I had never seen all of it because it had always been partly covered, and whenever I had pulled his balls out of his pants they had always made me smile, because they looked like the wrinkled face of an old man.

'Now, there was his cock reaching up towards his navel, majestic and nodding, and his balls tightly drawn up underneath it. Looking at them, my tummy went all watery and my knees went weak. He helped me into the shower beside him, and closed the door. There was so little room that we couldn't both stand there without brushing up against one another. If I was really turned on, he was, too. What really did for me was finding his rigid penis working against the top of my belly, and I began to grind myself against him. Within seconds I began to come off, and as I clung to him to steady the quivering of my orgasm, I felt his cock give several great throbs, and there was a searing sensation of warmth running down over my navel. He held me tightly to him and presently gave a great sigh, then went completely limp, and I felt my lips crushed under his.

'We stood under the shower for a minute or so longer, then he turned off the shower.

'As we stepped out he looked down at his cock, which had already gone quite limp, and said, "I've come!" "I know," I said. "So have I!" "I wanted to save it for later," he said. "He'll come up again if I have any say in the matter," I told him. His kissed me in the nape of my neck, sending a shiver all through me, and began to dry me. "You're a randy little darling, aren't you?" he said. "I like it," I said. "I know that! So do I! And you may be right!" he said. I was right, because when he had finished drying me, and I took the towel to do the same to him, his cock was already horizontal with the floor and by the time I had

finished it was pointing up to the ceiling again. Am I boring you, Dr Chartham?'

'Not at all!' I assured her.

She lit another cigarette.

'Do you remember your first fuck, Dr Chartham?' she asked.

'I'll never forget it,' I told her.

'How old were you?'

'Thirteen and a half.'

'Two years younger than us!' she exclaimed.

'But I had the great good luck to have a very experienced partner,' I told her, 'so that from the very first time it was so very good for me, and that, so I've learned, does not happen very often.'

'So I know now,' she agreed. 'Well, both of us were very lucky, Dr Chartham, because though it was the first time for David, too, it was fantastic for me, absolutely fantastic! And David has always said it was for him as well.'

'No pain?' I asked, professionally curious.

'No! David is well-hung, but not over-hung like Harry.'

'I didn't mean that,' I said.

'Oh, I see,' she said. 'No! Alice got rid of my hymen for me not long after we became – lovers, I suppose you'd have to call it. She hurt me then, but it wasn't too bad, and didn't last long.'

'I wish,' I began, then changed my mind. 'Never mind! Well, I'm glad it was so good for you.'

'We did have a bit of a shock, though,' she said. 'When we had sort of come back to earth, David suddenly put me aside and sat up. "Christ!" he said. "I've come in you! I forgot all about a french letter. I've got a packet in my room." He had taken me into his parents' room, saying the double bed would be more comfortable. "You're not due for your curse yet, are you?" he asked. "Another fortnight," I said, "but don't let's spoil it. If anything happens, it's too late now to do anything about it. Besides, I forgot, too, so I'm equally to blame." "I suppose you're right," he said, and we presently got turned on again, and the end of it

was just as beautiful and as satisfying. I often wonder, if we hadn't had it off that second time, whether I would have got pregnant. What do you think, Dr Chartham?'

'It's impossible to say,' I told her. 'I would think it wouldn't have made any difference. Were your periods regular then?'

'As clockwork, every 28 days.'

'So you would have been ovulating and really ripe for fertilisation.'

'I didn't know about ovulating then. No, that's a lie. You talk about it in *Mainly for Wives*, but I hadn't really understood.'

'It's more than likely that David's first emission was responsible, but it's not possible to say with certainty. There could have been a sperm in the second emission more speedy than any in the first emission.'

'Well, it doesn't really matter,' she smiled. 'Just a point of interest.'

Anyhow, a fortnight later – no period. And a month to six weeks later, morning sickness. 'And my nipples began to go a dark brown colour.'

The two children talked it over, and sensibly decided to take both sets of parents into their confidence straight away.

'Dad was great,' Janet said, 'but Mum took it hard for a couple of days. I'm sure it wasn't anything to do with what the neighbours would think, if you know what I mean, but how David and I were going to make out.'

'And David's parents?' I asked.

'David's dad was furious. "Why the bloody hell couldn't you have used a french letter? I thought you youngsters claim to be responsible?" But David's mum reminded him that he'd not been any more responsible, only luckier.'

All four parents and the two children had met to discuss what was best to be done.

'Dad asked if I wanted an abortion. David and I hadn't even thought of it! I said – rather pompously, I realise now – "My baby is a real love-baby! I don't want an abortion, I want a baby." David said he'd only agree to an abortion if it

proved impossible to work out a satisfactory plan for the immediate future, that is, for the time before he would be qualified and get a job and we could marry.

'Then David's father dropped the bombshell. "Has it occurred to anyone besides me," he asked, "that if the police get to know that Janet's pregnant, David could go to prison?" After cries of "Why?" from the women, David's dad said, "Because he's had unlawful intercourse with a girl of under the age of consent. Janet isn't 16 yet!"'

So now they really had to take notice of what the neighbours might say, in case the police found out.

So they planned. Janet was to go and live with her married sister in Southwold, in Suffolk. The school authorities were to be told that Janet was going to Southwold to be company for her sister, who was having a baby (true), while her trawler-master husband was at sea (also true), and that she would be attending a private school in Lowestoft (untrue). She and David were to marry at the register office in Felixstowe a week or two after her sixteenth birthday which, if calculations were correct, would be a few weeks before the baby would be born.

Fortunately, a few weeks after the situation, so to speak, 'broke', David had been accepted for a place at the North London Polytechnic. The two sets of parents decided that when the youngsters were married they would club together and buy them a small flat in Hampstead, where they could move after the baby had arrived and Janet felt confident enough to look after it.

'It all worked out very well,' Janet said. 'The first time I went home when the baby was about three months old, a few eyebrows were raised among the neighbours, but nothing was said. David got a bit frustrated when trying to study sometimes, when Martin fretted while cutting his teeth, but otherwise we were very, very happy – ecstatically so.

'Mum had seen to it that I was quite a good cook, and I enjoyed it and the housekeeping. Sometimes we were on the verge of running short, but our fathers chipped in and it was never very serious. My dad took to David wonderfully.

He'd always been disappointed that he and Mum hadn't had a son, and his contribution towards our housekeeping now and again somehow made him feel that David was more like a son than a son-in-law.'

'You were lucky,' I commented. 'Your parents have been very good to you.'

'I know that,' she said. 'We both do. If both lots hadn't been so understanding, it could have been ghastly. A couple of girls at school had "joined the club", and their parents had more or less kicked them out of the house. Yes, we still both appreciate how lucky we have been.'

'And what about sex?' I asked, because I was pretty certain that sex was at the root of the problem.

'Fantastic!' she exclaimed. 'Bloody fantastic! Before we got married, it was marvellous. David used to come to Southwold every Friday night to Monday morning, and until I got a bit too big and uncomfortable, we used to fuck ourselves silly. We had it away practically up to the end, from behind mostly, until the doctor said we ought to cut it down a bit, in case too many of my very strong orgasms too close together might bring me into premature labour. I don't know whether there's anything in that, or was he jealous, perhaps?'

'It was rather old-fashioned advice,' I remarked.

'David turned out to be frightfully randy. He could come two or three times in a couple of hours, and he was terribly adventurous. He was always wanting to try something new. We even got into the group scene as a regular pastime. After he qualified, he got a very good job with UVM, and he's had quite a few promotions in the short time he's been there. There were two or three junior executives at UVM who arranged the parties, and we got drawn in.'

I noticed that she had been speaking in the past tense, and drew her attention to it.

'Well, it is in the past,' she said.

'Perhaps you'll explain,' I suggested.

'Of course! About a year ago, David slowly began to go off sex, and after a few months he stopped making advances altogether. He'd play along if I started it, at least, at first he

would. Then after a time he began to make excuses for not doing even that.'

'What sort of excuses?' I asked. 'Did he plead tiredness?'

'No! I asked him why. Didn't he feel well, was he worried at work, was he having a bit on the side? . . . "No! No! No!" he said. I thought he was speaking the truth about not having a bit on the side because, before, not a single morning would pass without his waking up with a thumping erection, and now he didn't. He *used* to get a hard-on if he came into the bathroom when I was in the bath. But not any more! And until Harry came into my life and I tried to get him to satisfy me, it took me even longer and longer to get it up for him. Now I've given up altogether.'

'Doesn't he have any sex at all?' I said, puzzled.

'I've asked him outright more than once if he was wanking in secret. "No!" he said, and again I believe him. Besides he'd have to be doing it at work, because if he did it at home, I'd sense it – I'd know. I thought maybe he was ill. Under protest he went to the doctor – nothing wrong. But I made him take multivitamins, and I gave him several courses of natural Vitamin E *d'alphatercopherol*, as you suggest in one of your books . . .'

'Two or three,' I corrected her.

'Very good for general energy, you say. Well, not for David's! Several times I've asked him if he's gone off me, and he insists that he hasn't. I've thought about it and thought about it – and shed some tears about it, too – but I can't make out what's gone wrong. We've a nice house, nicely furnished, no money worries, and David's prospects are good. But lately I've been thinking it's not good enough.'

'I quite agree,' I said. 'I can't advise you really, without a chat with him. Would he come and see me?'

'I've asked him, but he's refused. I wanted him to come this afternoon, but he wouldn't. I've been wondering whether I should tell him I'm having it away with Harry?'

'What do you think his reaction would be?' I asked.

'Your guess is as good as mine. In his present mood I *think*, mind you, only *think*, that he wouldn't take any

notice of what I said. Probably wouldn't take it in. Haven't you got any ideas?'

'It could be an endocrine problem, that is, something may have affected the production of his sex-hormones, or it may be some deep psychological cause. In either case, we must have his co-operation if we're going to do any good.'

She sighed. 'What are we going to do?'

'What's his attitude towards the child?' I asked.

'Adores him! The only time I've seen him a bit put out was when his father bought Martin a very, very expensive toy.'

'Put out in what way?' I asked.

'When father-in-law had gone, all of a sudden, he burst out, "Does he bloody think I can't afford to buy my own son nice toys?" Does that help?'

'It tells us that he can have slightly jealous reactions towards Martin, though off-hand I couldn't say that his attitudes to the boy have any relation to his attitude towards you. What happened to you sex-wise before you met Harry?'

'Nothing that I didn't do myself. I'm not promiscuous by nature, Dr Chartham, but several months without any sexual contact with David was beginning to get me down. That's when I used to cry, sometimes for hours on end when I was on my own.'

'How did you meet Harry?' I asked.

'By chance, really. I've made a few good friends in our age-group in Hampstead. One or two of the girls realised something wasn't quite right, and asked what was wrong, but I couldn't talk to them about it.'

'Why not?'

'I felt it would be disloyal to David.'

'More disloyal than having it away with Harry?'

'I'd never thought of having it away with anyone then. In fact, getting it together with Harry initially was a sort of spur-of-the-moment thing. These friends began to ask me to go round and see them in the evening, and David did nothing but sit in front of the TV, so I asked him if he'd mind if I accepted these invitations. He said no, he'd be

pleased for me to get out of the house. Recently I've thought that this attitude of his must be more physical than psychological.

'Well, I went round to Grant and Audrey's one evening and Harry was there. He's Grant's cousin, though Grant is a bit embarrassed by his appearance. Audrey said Grant had come in slightly sloshed, and they were both, well, all three, quite merry by the time I got there. I don't know whether there's anything going between Grant and Harry. I'll ask Harry one day.

'Anyhow, while we were having a bit of a giggle about something, Grant suddenly said, slurring his "esses", "It's ridiculous, you know. There's Janet aching for cock, and there's Harry with that huge great weapon and nowhere for it to go. Why don't we have a sex knees-up, just the four of us?" "Not in cold blood," said Audrey. "I'm not quite so sloshed as that! I know, let's play strip-poker, to warm up." So we did. I'm no good at poker at the best of times, and I was soon in the raw. Grant was really too pissed to make any real go at the game, and soon he was sitting opposite me, starkers. Then Audrey and Harry had a bit of a ding-dong, which Audrey lost. So there we were, three of us completely nude, and Harry down to his socks and Y-fronts. There was a big bulge in his pants, and Audrey and I were so taken by surprise when Harry stood up and began to wriggle out of them, that Audrey collapsed with a little shriek, covering her eyes with her hand. "There you are!" exclaimed Grant. "What did I tell you? Ever seen such a beautiful rod? Come here, my darling!" and he lurched towards Audrey and they were soon hard at it.

'Believe me, Dr Chartham, that dong of Harry's is immense. It's not only long but very thick as well. I was mesmerised by it and couldn't resist making friends with it. Harry wasn't a sophisticated lover, but he had been around. In any case I was well and truly turned on . . . Well, you don't want the details. I'd never have believed what it means to be so completely filled as that. I came and came and came!'

'As a matter of interest,' I asked, 'does a large penis do anything special for you?'

'I've thought about it a bit, and I've decided that David's which is three-and-a-half inches shorter, and one-and-a-half inches slimmer, used to do more for me than this vast rod. I said just now that there's magic in it, and so there is. But I think that most of the magic is in my mind.'

'In my mind!' The phrase kept churning round in my mind as she chatted away, until I found myself thinking that David's was really a psychological problem. Perhaps what he needed was some shock treatment! The more I thought about it, the more convinced I became that I was right.

I explained to Janet what I thought.

'Would Harry play along, do you think?' I asked.

'Let's ask him,' she suggested.

So she fetched him and told him what I had just suggested.

'Yeah!' said afro-haired Harry. 'I'm game, if it's going to make Janet happy.'

'If it works,' I warned him, while Janet was freshening up in the bathroom, 'you're pretty sure to lose her.'

'Don't worry about that, Doc!' he smiled. 'I don't have any trouble getting my rocks off. If it makes David come out of his fucking trance, it'll be my good deed to society. Would you like to add me to your statistical collection?'

'If you're agreeable,' I said. So we made a date for a small scientific investigation for the following week.

'Did it work?' I asked him.

'Like a dream, Doc! The only thing was, he threw me out of the house bollock naked, and there I was shivering in the garden until Janet threw my clothes out of the sitting-room window to me!'